They came to Glengallan

A family history

Also by Jenny Kroonstuiver:

Glimpses of Jean: The story of Jean Zuvela-Doda

Winton: The Swann Family Story

They came to Glengallan

A family history

Jenny Kroonstuiver

This is an IndieMosh book

brought to you by MoshPit Publishing
an imprint of Mosher's Business Support Pty Ltd

PO Box 4363
Penrith NSW 2750

indiemosh.com.au

 A catalogue record for this
work is available from the
National Library of Australia

NATIONAL
LIBRARY
OF AUSTRALIA

https://www.nla.gov.au/collections

Title:	They came to Glengallan
Subtitle:	A family history
Author:	Kroonstuiver, Jenny
ISBNs:	978-1-922628-21-3 (paperback)
Subjects:	HISTORY: Australia & New Zealand; HISTORY: Social History; BIOGRAPHY & AUTOBIOGRAPHY / General SOCIAL SCIENCE: Sociology / Rural

The author has made every effort to ensure that the information in this book
was correct at the time of publication. However, the author and publisher
accept no liability for any loss, damage or disruption incurred by the reader or
any other person arising from any action taken or not taken based on the
content of this book. The author recommends seeking third party advice and
considering all options prior to making any decision or taking action in regard
to the content of this book.

Cover images supplied by Jenny Kroonstuiver; background images of sky and
paper used under licence from Envato Elements

Cover design and layout by Ally Mosher at allymosher.com

Contents

Introduction

One of my most enduring childhood memories relates to the way my mother served dinner on the sheep station. We had a white lace tablecloth, carefully laid polished silver cutlery with bone handles (we were taught from a very young age how to lay the cutlery correctly), crisply starched white serviettes in serviette rings and placemats for the hot dishes. The placemats were pictures from the previous year's calendars, each carefully pasted onto a piece of rounded Masonite and then varnished: selecting new pictures and updating the placemats was a favoured January job for we children.

Dinner was always served at the table. Dad carved the meat from the head of the table, and each plate was passed down the table to my mother at the other end for a serving of vegetables and gravy. Mum had a series of matching serving dishes, including a polished silver warming dish which I still have and cherish.

Correct table manners were instilled into us from an early age. Seating was carefully ordered, we never began to eat until everyone was served, and no-one ever, ever left the table until everyone had finished.

When I look back now, I often think it must have been almost incongruous for visitors, thinking they had travelled into the wild outback, only to be greeted with more dinner formality than many had ever experienced. As children we never questioned these dinner traditions, but with the benefit of age I can now see that they were a reflection of my mother's own upbringing.

I had not appreciated, until researching for this book, just how much a part of the Queensland squattocracy my mother's family was. Many branches of her family were closely involved in the settlement of the Darling Downs and western Queensland. Financed by wealthy Scottish financiers and riding high on the early wealth generated from the wool industry, they established new stations throughout the region. Many of them went on to become magistrates, bankers and well-established community leaders.

They had their share of problems, though – several experienced foreclosures or bankruptcy, but quickly recovered to continue their pioneering ways. In their later years many gravitated to the area around Warwick, Kingaroy and Nanango, or moved to Brisbane.

For some, this was a transition to wealth in a single generation. Families such as the Whites and Pointons had left situations of poverty and starvation in Staffordshire in the mid-19th century, looking for a new life and fresh opportunities. With little money and large families, they joined thousands of people travelling to Australia, attracted by stories of gold, wool and wealth.

Other members of our family came from surprisingly affluent backgrounds. They were not 'old money', but part of a new generation of wealthy merchants that had capitalised on the industrial changes which occurred so rapidly in the early 19th century. For families such as the Lees, Deuchars and Allans, Australia offered new challenges, as well as the promise of great wealth and adventure. These were the families who came to Glengallan, the beautiful homestead which was the site of so many significant family events during the mid-late 19th century.

They were willing to work hard, take risks and head out to unknown areas of Queensland in search of new opportunities. And many of them succeeded. Some are recorded in the Australian Stockmen's Hall of Fame; they were staunch supporters of separation from NSW and members of the Nationalist Party; and many became household names across the colony.

Most telling was the fact that I managed to flesh out much of my Grandmother's early years from the social pages of the Brisbane newspapers. Her war work, social engagements and charity work were reported almost weekly.

Several generations later, the wealth was gone but the legacy remained. I can understand now why my own mother, a trained mothercraft nurse, was instantly drawn to work in western Queensland. There she met my father, and their own life together is the story of a new generation of pioneers, as they established a huge sheep station in Western Australia.

This book includes her story, in her own words. In her later years, Ruth Lee had Parkinson's Disease, and lost the power to write and eventually to even speak. However, early in her retirement she typed as much as she could onto an old typewriter, and this gave me a wonderful foundation to work from.

Ruth also researched much of her family history and left for me a pile of birth and death certificates she had obtained as well as stories, letters, photos and records. Her sister, Nancy, had left a similar cache to her daughter Yvette, to whom I am greatly indebted. Yvette's collaboration, support and willingness to scour old records has provided an invaluable trove of information. It was gratifying to see that in the process she caught the family history 'bug' and began researching her father's family. A further contributor was a descendant of Albert Pointon, Sally Chapman, who had inherited many of the Pointon photographs and records and who had also undertaken a significant amount of family research herself. I am indebted to Sally for her advice and contributions.

Jenny Kroonstuiver

Tracing the stories of one's ancestors, while fascinating, is a humbling experience. To see the hardships and challenges they experienced, and how much their lives were shaped by historical events, is illuminating. Our own sense of self-importance is so quickly tempered when we learn of our origins.

This is why it is so important that these stories are recorded for the next generation. Most of them will not appreciate the value of records such as these until they are older, but it is there for them when they are ready to.

Glengallan

Where the bold mountains lift their rugged heads,
Keeping still guard o'er Millar's happy vale
And lonely Sturt his sullen shadow sheds,
Braving the Christmas sun and wintry gale, –
And lowing herds adorn the peaceful dale,
Answer the bleatings of the timid ewe.
Luring her sportive young with plaintive wail –
Behold! Glengallan bursts upon the view,
To weary wanderers a beacon kind and true.

There live generous hearts, whose pulses beat
With the warm blood of old McCullamore, –
That warlike race who never knew defeat,
But stretch'd their conquering arms from shore to shore,
Holding with dauntless heart and stout claymore,
The right o'er glen and mountain, loch and isle –
Their might with years increasing more and more,
Till monarchs bent to gain their fav'ring smile,
And startled foemen shook at thy dread name – Argyle!

But it may be that in this sunny land
Their thoughts to scenes of purer joy may roam:
To childhood's hours, when, wand'ring hand in hand,
They trod the heather of their mountain home;
Unbidden recollections onward come –
The bounding lake, with white sails dotted o'er,
The falling waters flashing in the sun,
Bursting in clouds of foam above Glenmore,
And mimicking in sport old ocean's distant roar.

Honor'd supporters of a noble name!
'Midst all thy worth thy greatest boast shall be,
The heritage of blood remains the same
From the great founder of thy race to thee –
The same old Highland Hospitality –

Jenny Kroonstuiver

Not pausing when the traveller's at the door,
Because he may not be of thy degree;
But sheltering all, as did thy sires of yore,
Shall make Glenagallan's fame coeval with Glenmore.

W.W.
Brisbane, October 20, 1846
This poem was published as original poetry in the Moreton
Bay Courier on Saturday 31 October 1846

Places of significance – Australia

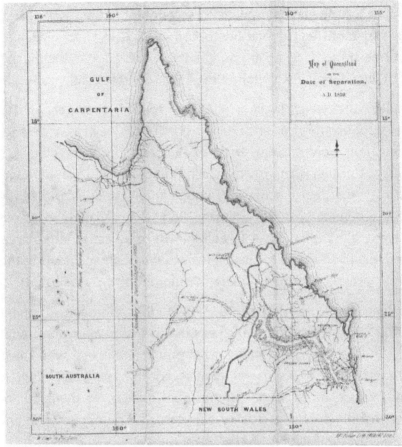

Map of Queensland at Separation in 1859[i]

The Hunter Valley, NSW

Lochinvar in the Hunter Valley was the place where several of our Scottish ancestors first arrived, due to their association with the North British Australasian Loan and Investment Co, or the 'Aberdeen Company'. This company was formed in Aberdeen, Scotland, in 1839 and had raised an initial sum of £50,000 (roughly

$1.4m today) for investment in the colonies. Loans were to be advanced to land buyers and crown lands were to be purchased for the company. Shortly after its founding, a land surveyor named James Forbes Beattie was sent to NSW as the British company's manager in the colonies, with an accountant named John Rae as his assistant. Beattie had been born in 1801 in Kincardineshire, and he brought Scottish immigrants to NSW for the company, including our ancestors John Deuchar and Hugh Allan.

Today, the New England Highway follows the track which developed initially as a stock route north from Newcastle to reach the prime wool growing areas of the New England region, and passes through many towns which reflect this Scottish heritage, such as Aberdeen, Lochinvar, Dundee and Glen Innes. During the 1860s, several robberies occurred along the road, with infamous bushranger Captain Thunderbolt known to be active in the area. Archibald Lee refers to the theft of Wallumbilla mail during this time, but it is not known whether Thunderbolt was the culprit.

During the depression of 1843-1844, the Aberdeen Company came into possession of much pastoral land and many thousands of sheep in NSW, but generally the policy followed with these properties was to dispose of them as quickly as possible to buyers and, where this was out of the question, to let them out to dependable people at a fairly high rental. By the mid-1850s the company was acting purely as a mortgage and investment concern.

The exceedingly high price of Australian wool in the 1860s encouraged the company to enter the farming field as a period of considerable pastoral expansion began in Australia. Subsequently, they invested heavily in the development of the Darling Downs, Maranoa and the Gulf country. When wool prices suddenly crashed in 1866, many graziers went under and, because of foreclosures, the company suddenly found itself the owner of a significant number of pastoral runs. Restructuring, consolidation and greater efficiencies such as fencing improvements and the introduction of Kanaka labour in the Gulf country during the 1870s saw a slow recovery.

The Darling Downs

The Darling Downs is a farming region on the western slopes of the Great Dividing Range in southern Queensland, Australia. The Downs are to the west of South East Queensland and are one of the major regions of Queensland. The name was generally applied to an area approximating to that of the Condamine River catchment upstream of Condamine township but is now applied to a wider region comprising the Southern Downs, Western Downs, Toowoomba and Goondiwindi local authority areas. The name 'Darling Downs' was given in 1827 by Allan Cunningham, the first European explorer to reach the area and the name was in recognition of the then Governor of New South Wales, Ralph Darling.

Baranggum is an Australian Aboriginal language spoken by the Baranggum people and their language region includes the landscape within the local government boundaries of the Western Downs Regional Council, particularly Dalby, Tara, Jandowae and west towards Chinchilla.

Originally, the Darling Downs was covered with a wealth of indigenous grasses which created ideal vegetation for stock for most of the year. The Darling Downs Aborigines had an annual burning season at the time when the indigenous grasses were ripe and dry. These annual fires gave the local Aborigines of the Darling Downs the name 'Goonneeburra' and this is how Downs tribes were known to the coastal Aborigines who inhabited the Moreton Bay area. The Goonneeburra were once situated where Warwick stands today.

Allan Cunningham set out to explore the area to the west of Moreton Bay in 1827, crossing to the west of the Great Dividing Range from the Hunter Region and travelling north. In June 1827, Cunningham climbed to the top of Mount Dumaresq and wrote in his diary that this lush area was ideal for settlement. Exploring around Mount Dumaresq, Cunningham also found a pass, now known as Cunninghams Gap.

News of the lush pastures quickly spread, resulting in a land grab that authorities in the distant NSW colony found difficult to control. Many of these new arrivals were members of a privileged society, younger sons of the English and Scottish gentry, who were obliged to leave home and travel far away in order to make a living. Several of these young men were our ancestors. The first to come north were Patrick Leslie and his brother Walter in 1846, sons of a Scottish laird who settled at Canning Downs on the Condamine River. Leslie belonged to a well-known family of that name, from the estate of Wartle of Aberdeenshire, Scotland. We have links (but not familial) to the Leslie family through both the Deuchars and the Allans.

On September 9, 1840, Patrick Leslie was married to one of the daughters of Hannibal Macarthur, of Parramatta, and his brother George married another Macarthur daughter at about the same time. These women, as with many other subsequent pioneer women, needed permission from the NSW government to come through Brisbane, which was at that time a penal settlement, and rode their horses through Cunninghams Gap to their homes on the Darling Downs. They were relatives of Captain John Macarthur, who took such a prominent and distinguished part in helping to lay the foundations of the Australian merino wool industry and also of viticulture.

The Leslies originally owned land that they later sold to the Campbell brothers and which became Glangallan Station, which played such a central role in our family history. It was the Campbells who named the area 'Glengallan', after a district in their home of Perthshire in Scotland. The Leslies also sold Rosenthal Creek to the Aberdeen Company, which later became the North British Australasian Company, with which many of our ancestors had a connection, including John Deuchar and Hugh Allan. John Deuchar managed Rosenthal before moving on to Glengallan.

The Campbell Bros sold Glengallan to Charles Marshall, an Englishman, and in 1855 John Deuchar bought into this property. Deuchar was then manager of Rosenthal, and superintendent of the North British Australasian Company's properties, a position he retained. He was still at Rosenthal when he married 16-year-old Eliza Lee in 1857. The Glengallan Merino Stud soon became famous for producing high-class sheep, having the blend of the Negrette and Rambouillet strains. In 1867 John Deuchar built the handsome house at Glengallan, where he and his family resided for many years.

Other well-established residences on the southern downs include the Talgai Homestead, Pringle Cottage and Rosenthal Homestead. It is interesting to note that the beautiful old homestead of Rosenthal, built by Fred Bracker, was recently featured in the ABC television series *Restoration Australia*. It is also rumoured that the bushranger Captain Thunderbolt worked there on occasion.

One of the first stations to be established was Jimbour House. It was also the point from where Ludwig Leichhardt launched his fateful expedition to the Northern Territory in 1844.

The homes which the first squatters constructed were modest slab huts not far removed from the canvas or iron huts of their employees. However, after legal changes in the late 1840s permitted the purchase of pastoral leases, the squatters began to establish a more permanent and impressive presence.

By 1844 there twenty-six properties including several sheep stations with more than 150,000 sheep in total. This first generation of squatters formed a close-knit community who shared the same values and interests and sealed their associations by intermarrying. Local Aboriginals and European squatters co-settled the area from the late 1840s onwards. The Darling Downs then became known as the 'jewel in the diadem of squatterdom' with an elite 'pure merino' class living in comfortable houses.

> "The normal traveller comes out with introductions to the gentlemen of the colony, and the gentlemen of the colony are squatters. The squatters' houses are open to him. They introduce the traveller to their clubs. They lend their horses and buggies. Their wives and daughters are pretty and agreeable. They exercise all the duties of hospitality with a free hand. They get up kangaroo hunts and make picnics. It is always pleasant to sympathize with an aristocracy when an aristocracy will open its arms to you."
>
> Anthony Trollope, Australia and New Zealand, Authorized Australian Edition, 1876, p.24.

The grandest of the Darling Downs houses was John Deuchar's Glengallan, a two-storey stone homestead in the plantation style, constructed near Warwick in 1867. Features included a ballroom, especially commissioned furniture and a bathroom with the most modern amenities including running water pumped from the Condamine River. The money to build on such a scale came from giant wool cheques (50 per cent of a wool clip was clear profit in the 1870s) and from generous lines of bank credit.

Only one wing was ever completed. After John Deuchar's death, the homestead, incomplete and inadequate, eventually became derelict, seemingly beyond repair. The once-great Glengallan went into a decline lasting more than 70 years during which furniture and fittings were sold or removed from the building. The house survived the post-war threat of demolition, but the ravages of time and neglect took a dreadful toll. Now a team of volunteers is gradually restoring the house, which stands majestically amid paddocks of sunflowers and other crops. The sensitive restoration work carried out by this group enables visitors to appreciate the original attractiveness of this home.

About 1875[ii]

With wool prices rising, the squatters sought political power and lobbied to bring about separation of the northern district from NSW. In the early 1850s there was an intense struggle for the separation of the northern part of NSW, to make it into another state. Among the members of the most determined group were Patrick Leslie and Arthur Hodgson, the men who were the first to settle on the Darling Downs. They were opposed by those who still wished to have access to ticket-of-leave labour. Queensland was finally gazetted in 1859.

The way of life established by the 'Shepherd Kings' of the Darling Downs lasted less than 50 years. Throughout the second half of the 19th century, they were faced with changing political attitudes, as successive governments introduced land acts designed to reduce their enormous holdings in support of closer agricultural settlement.

In 1854, Charles Douglas Eastaughffe, later a police trooper and chief constable of Dalby, settled in the area. Spicers Gap Road opened up the area in the 1850s. Later, the expansion of Queensland Rail's train networks and Cobb & Co's stagecoach transport greatly assisted with access to the region. Gold was found in the district around this time, but it was agriculture that provided for the boom times ahead.

Financially, the pastoralists were dependent on a system which could not continually promise them a rich living. Up until 1866, profits from both wool and cattle were high. Then, following a depression which led to the loss of Wallumbilla by Archibald Lee, there was another period of prosperity that lasted from 1871 to 1877. After these good times, the pastoral industry began to change irrevocably. Affected by droughts and floods, poor seasons and increased costs, the properties became a burden: funds dried up (especially in the 1890s) and sheep and cattle production became much less profitable.

The 1891 Australian shearers' strike started at Jondaryan. This strike is one of Australia's earliest and most important industrial disputes. It was primarily between unionised and non-unionised wool workers and resulted in the formation of large camps of striking workers, and had minor instances of sabotage and violence on both sides. The strike was poorly timed and, when the union workers ran out of food, they were forced to come to terms. The outcome is credited as being one of the factors for the formation of the Australian Labor Party. The Brisbane Courier reported that, despite the strike, Glengallan shearing was progressing well in the hands of five unionists and several learners.

During the early 20th century, dairy was a significant industry for Queensland. The 1930s saw the peaking of it on the Downs, with 6500 farms and more than 200,000 milking cows. The Downs Co-operative Dairy Association expanded, constructed or bought at least 10 butter and cheese factories across the Darling Downs. The Downs Co-operative Dairy Association Ltd factory in Toowoomba closed in 2006.

The Darling Downs experienced a water crisis as the Condamine River dried up during the severe drought of 1994/1995.

In 2010, the population of the Darling Downs was estimated to be 241,537 people.

Warwick

With the pulse of settlement becoming stronger every day, the NSW government saw the advantage of forming a town on part of the Canning Downs run and, in 1847, decided that Patrick Leslie should select the site – this was to become Warwick. It was established in the 1850s, and the first allotment was bought by Leslie. After the first business places had been established in Warwick, most married people on adjoining stations bought land in town and built houses for their families.

Eliza Deuchar's brother, Washington Lee, was practicing as doctor in Warwick in 1869 and, at about the same time, her other brother and our ancestor, Archibald Lee, also lived there after leaving Wallumbilla. His only daughter was born in Warwick.

Warwick East state school opened on 4 November 1850 and is one of the oldest state primary schools in Queensland. A Presbyterian church was built in 1858 and the telegraph to Brisbane was operating by 1861.

The 1870s were boom years for this new town. In 1871, the railway reached Warwick, a brewery was built in 1873, then a cooperative flour mill and brickworks were built in 1874. A hospital was built in the early 1880s.

Today, Warwick is the administrative centre of the Southern Downs region local government area.

Ipswich

Ipswich began in 1827 as a limestone-mining settlement and convict outstation and grew rapidly as a major inland port. Ipswich was initially named 'The Limestone Hills', later abbreviated to 'Limestone', but in 1843 it was renamed after the town of Ipswich in England.

By 1830, convicts were quarrying limestone and a kiln was built that produced 300-400 baskets of lime a week. The lime was mixed with mortar to build Brisbane's stone buildings.

In 1836, a government station was established at Redbank. It bred sheep and cattle and, in 1838, George Thorn, who arrived in the area to take charge of the government's cattle, sheep and horses, became Ipswich's first free settler.

By 1840, a small settlement, nothing more than a couple of houses and a general store, had been established in the area. From the 1840s on, as squatters rapidly took up land in the area, coal was discovered at Redbank, and development of the township was rapid.

The boiling-down works, the 'Warrell Steaming Establishment', operated by our ancestor Hugh Allan, was established at Warrell, about two miles south of Ipswich, in 1846. Ipswich was proclaimed a municipality in 1860 and the railway to Brisbane was completed in 1876.

It was during the 1860s that Archibald Lee began buying goods from Wilson & Co in Ipswich, an association that lasted for more than 20 years. George Harrison Wilson founded GH Wilson & Co in Ipswich in about 1853. The merchant business was run by George Wilson for at least 40 years.

By 1904, Ipswich had become a city and had a population of 8637.

Maranoa region

The Gunggari language region of South West Queensland includes the landscape within the local government boundaries of the Maranoa Region particularly the towns of Mitchell, Amby, Dunkeld and Mungallala and the properties of Forest Vale and North Yanco.

Gungabula is an Australian Aboriginal language of the headwaters of the Dawson River in Central Queensland. The language region includes areas within the local government area of Maranoa Region, particularly the towns of Charleville, Augathella and Blackall and as well as the Carnarvon Range.

One of the best sources of information about the European settlement of this area comes from a publication *Reminiscences of the Early Settlement of the Maranoa District* published by Mary McManus in 1903[1]. Mary's family lived at Mt Abundance, which her father Stephen Spencer had purchased in 1857. He arrived in 1858, after four months on the road, with his wife and two

---

[1] Mary A McManus (1902) *Reminiscences of the Early Settlement of the Maranoa District*, A Project Gutenberg of Australia eBook

children, thirteen men, 1,000 head of cattle, 60 horses, 4 laden bullock drays and a spring cart in which his family travelled.

Along the way they stopped at other newly established stations including Nindigully, Boomba, and St George's Bridge where the town of St George now stands. They then camped for some time at Warroo and Wargoo Stations, the property of Mr. Robert Fitzgerald, a wealthy squatter of New South Wales, then No. Ten, Mr. Becket's Station, and from there onto Donga station. Other stops included Werribene and Talavera.

> "My mother was the first squatter's wife who ever came into the Maranoa district, and my brother and I were the first children. It was a rough life we had then. My mother was quite unused to it, and I was too young to be of much assistance to her. No household servants would venture out then, no matter what inducement was held out to them. We were obliged to perform all our household duties as best we could. We lived in this great tent, in which all our cooking utensils and cases of household effects were stored away, so there was not much room to spare. Here I made my first damper, which was by no means a success. The weather too was bitterly cold. The water in the buckets was almost solid ice. We turned it out the shape of the buckets."

Stephen Spencer decided to build the head station on the banks of the Bungeworgorai Creek, which was about 50 miles west of Wallumbilla Station, which at that time was owned by William Gordon.

In 1859 Queensland separated from New South Wales, resulting in a rush for taking up new country and exploring expeditions, which continued until 1864. Mary McManus recalled:

"The excitement was extreme, and nearly equal to that of the gold rush seven or eight years before. As before said, Mount Abundance was the furthest out station in a westerly direction, consequently it formed a depot for all explorers both going out and coming in, it being the only store where supplies could be obtained."

Mary McManus recalls that Kilmorey Run was taken up in May 1861, by George Deuchar and Archibald Lee, who also took delivery of Wallumbilla in March 1862.

"In 1863, Mr. Lee took their first sheep out, and formed the station, erecting huts and sheepyards, and later in the year he camped there under a small tent with Mrs. Lee for the shearing. Mr. Lee married Miss M. Allan, Mr. G. Deuchar's niece. Mr. G. Deuchar was brother to Mr. John Deuchar, formerly a partner with Mr. Marshall of Glengallan, near Warwick. In 1864 Mr. Deuchar went to reside permanently at Kilmorey, where he lived for several years. He died in 1890 at Stanthorpe."

Roma

Mt Abundance, the home of Mary McManus, was only a few miles from the site of the town to become Roma. With the opening of the Bowen Hotel, Roma sprang into existence. Most of the surrounding area was very thickly timbered, and scrub had to be cut down to clear a place to build the Bowen Hotel. The Maranoa Hotel was built soon afterwards by a man named Mazareth, and Thomas Reid moved his hotel from near the old crossing to Roma. Thus, there were three public houses standing almost together before there was a single private residence. A court of petty sessions was established soon afterwards, together with police quarters. The post office was moved from Mt Abundance station to Roma.

The establishment of the lands office at Roma was welcomed by all squatters and explorers, who before then had lost much valuable time travelling to St George.

The first stores were opened in 1863. The first chemist was George Ellis, and the first saddler was Mr LC Johnson. Dr Edward Moran came to Roma in about 1863 and was the first medical man to resided there permanently.

Roma was named in honour of Lady Bowen, wife of Queensland's first governor. She was a Greek woman whose maiden name was Roma Diamentina, the latter name given to the Queensland western river Diamentina, which flows into Lake Eyre. In 1874, a sketch of Roma showed a post and telegraph office, police station, and about a dozen houses. It became a municipality on 25 May 1867, lapsed in 1875, and was re-established in 1876.

Warrego District

The Warrego district stretches from the western parts of the Darling Downs to the South Australian border. Along the Balonne Highway it runs from St George to Cunnamulla and on to Thargomindah. It also stretches along the Warrego Highway from Roma to Charleville, and in between stretches east from Surat through Tara to Dalby.

The Warrego runs were taken up and occupied simultaneously with those in the Maranoa.

Dulbydilla (or 'Black's Waterhole', as Mary McManus claimed it was generally called) was taken up by John Charles McManus in 1862, and afterwards forfeited by him. Then William Burton bought it at government auction and built a hotel there, which he called The Traveller's Rest. For some years it was the only house of any kind on the road from Mitchell to Charleville (a distance of 120 miles). For some reason, Burton did not succeed there, and he sold the house and run to Messrs Pettiford and Anderson, who, in their turn, disposed of it to Mr John McKenzie, who converted it into a private residence.

The next station on the Charleville road to be taken up in about 1862 was Eurella by Captain T. J. Saddler, near where the town of Morven now stands. For some years Morven was known as 'Saddler's Waterhole', as it was there that the captain and his wife were camped for some time whilst their house was being built four miles below Morven on the main road to Charleville.

Maryvale was taken up and formed by AF Surlick, who named the place after his wife. He also took up and formed Mt Maria, also naming this place after his wife, whose name was Mary. Mt Maria later became the property of Robert Douglas, the husband of our ancestor Hugh Allan's daughter Mary Ann.

The floods of 1864 not only swamped Brisbane, but large areas of western Queensland. The area between the Balonne and Moonie rivers, over 50km apart, were as one for hundreds of miles after the Maranoa and other rivers and creeks joined them. These lands were completely inundated for some time after the rain had ceased.

Despite calamitous weather, Mary McManus provided a delightful description of the clothes women of western Queensland wore for 'good wear'.

> "As for the ladies, they wore the crinolines of the most ample dimensions, and small pork-pie hats. Also Garibaldi jackets (now called blouses). Brown holland was seen everywhere, and everything was made of and covered with it, even to our hats. Hats too, were trimmed with large streamers of several colours of

ribbon, reaching to the feet behind, and we wore velvet neck ribbons also tied with long streamers down our back. Our hair was dressed down over our ears, bulged out on each side with pads made of various materials with a huge bow behind with long ends of ribbon reaching to our feet, to say nothing of the heavy chenille hair nets of black and every other colour, some large enough to hold a large cabbage."

However, there was not a great deal of regular social interaction as most properties were a considerable distance apart. Despite this there was a sense of comradeship and fellowship amongst the settlers.

Morven

Morven is named from Morven, a round-topped mountain in Aberdeenshire. The first store was started about 1878, and it quickly became a prosperous place, the depot for a rich pastoral country and stations such as: Ularunda, Chance Downs, Maryvale, Brunell, Mount Maria, Angellala, Burenda, Victoria Downs, Ivanhoe, Alice Downs, and Armadilla.

In the late 1950s, Ruth and Eric Swann managed Tatala Station, which was midway between Charleville and Morven. As a child of eight at the time, I have some quite clear memories of this station, including the pisé house, frogs and snakes seeking refuge from the flooded nearby Nebine Creek, and of swagmen who frequently called and performed odd jobs in exchange for meat and potatoes. The open-air picture theatre on the banks of the Nebine Creek and closer to Charleville was built by my father and his neighbours in about 1960 and is still in use today.

Charleville

Charleville was surveyed and named by surveyor Tully (afterwards surveyor-general of Queensland), and he named it from the Charleville in his native county of Cork, Ireland. There is also a town of the same name in France. The site was originally part of old Gowrie Station and the town is the centre of an extensive pastoral district, servicing stations such as: Arabella, Riversleigh, Nive Junction, Wellwater, Burrendilla, Dillaba, Mt Morris, Oakwood, and Yarran Vale.

This was the main supply town for Eric and Ruth Swann when they were at Tatala Station. My sister Susan was born in Charleville.

Yaraka

Yaraka is located 220 kilometres south of Longreach, 165 kilometres west of Blackall and 100 kilometres south of the town of Isisford.

Yaraka has a fascinating history that covers the early settlers from the 1860s, the railway, the balloting of settlement blocks and the wool industry. Yaraka also has a unique history with Queensland Rail and is famous amongst rail enthusiasts as being 'Yaraka – the end of the line'. There are a number of stories as to why the line abruptly ended at Yaraka.

The Yaraka area was once part of the giant Milo sheep station located on the southern side of the Yang Yang Ranges. Yaraka was one of their huge paddocks where vast numbers of Merino sheep grazed and produced much sought-after low micron wool. The state Government split up the Milo leases thus allowing the early settlers to become 'kings and queens' of their own properties.

This was where Ruth Lee was sent in 1947 on her first mothercraft nurse placement at Retreat Station, and was also where she met her future husband Eric Swann. She later returned to work at Mt Marlow Station.

Blackall

Blackall is 964km north-west of Brisbane. This is where Ruth and Eric Swann's first three children, Jenny, David and Russell, were born.

European settlers first moved into the area in 1864 and, in 1868, a township was surveyed and named after Samuel Wensley Blackall, governor of Queensland from 1868 to 1871.

Blade shearer Jack Howe put Blackall on the map in 1892 at nearby Alice Downs Station when he set a world record by shearing 321 sheep in seven hours and 40 minutes. It took another 58 years before anyone matched this feat and that was with machine shears. Jack Howe is memorialised in a bronze sculpture that can be viewed when wandering along the Shamrock Stroll, a historical walk around the town.

The first artesian bore in the outback was drilled in Blackall in 1885 and today visitors can rest, relax and revive in the natural artesian waters at the Blackall Aquatic Centre's thermal spa and swimming pool.

Blackall (as with Merriwagga in NSW) claims to be the home of the Black Stump, which was used for surveying purposes and permanently marks the original Astro Station established in 1887. Anything west of this point is said to be 'beyond the black stump'.

This was the location of the nearest hospital to Mt Marlow Station, which is where Eric and Ruth Swann were living when I was born in 1954.

Areas around Brisbane

Doughboy Creek/Hemmant

First named Bulimba Creek, it was renamed Doughboy Creek in 1866 and Hemmant in 1878. The creek itself is a perennial stream that is a tributary of the Brisbane River, and the area is now in suburban Brisbane.

The whole district had been named after William Hemmant, a local parliamentarian, in 1876. He was treasurer in the Macalister government and between 1873 and 1876 represented the Bulimba electorate.

The first land sales took place in 1858. The soil was fertile and easy to clear, and the first crops were vegetables and fruit, which were transported up the river to Brisbane until the construction of the bridge over Bulimba Creek in 1870 made road transport possible – this bridge was later the site of the tragic death of Frederick Joyce.

The Tingalpa district, which includes Hemmant, opened to farming in 1859. Settlement expanded following the introduction of the 1864 coffee and sugar regulations, when most of the land in the district along Doughboy Creek (Bulimba Creek) and the Brisbane River was taken up for sugar growing. A Wesleyan church was opened in November 1866.

Hemmant State school was established in 1864 as the Bulimba Creek school. The now heritage-listed replacement building commenced in 1876 and is one of several generations of public works buildings that were built as the community at Hemmant expanded and developed.

In 1863, William Gibson and his son Angus arrived in Moreton Bay and settled at Hemmant. The remainder of the family followed in 1864. In 1866, William Gibson obtained cane cuttings from Louis Hope at Ormiston, which he planted at Hemmant on a farm he called Clydesdale. Other farmers in the district also switched to sugar production. In 1868, William Gibson & Sons established the Clydesdale sugar mill, and the prospect of employment at the mill would be what enticed our ancestor, Joseph White, to stop here in 1867 instead of going on to Bundaberg as he originally planned.

Hemmant is also where the Pointon family first settled after they arrived in Brisbane in the 1860s. The Balmoral cemetery was originally called the Kangaroo Point Burial Ground and the first burial was believed to have taken place in 1874. Sadly, it was that of George Wilson Pointon, a six-year-old lad who had drowned in Norman Creek on 26 June 1874. His brother William was disinterred from the Brisbane cemetery (Lang Park) and reinterred with him. Their parents, William and Annie Pointon, are also buried in the same gravesite, which is close to the cemetery gates.

By 1871 there were seven mills in the area. In the second half of the 1870s, however, drought and disease destroyed crops repeatedly and sugar farming was moved further north. In 1883, the Clydesdale mill was sold, and the Gibson family moved to Bingera at Bundaberg. The mill closed the following year, and Hemmant returned to vegetable and dairy production.

Strathpine

Originally a farming community, Strathpine was named by the Railways Department in 1887, when a distinctive name was sought for the railway station, which was to be brought into service the following year.

Previously known as the 'North Pine' settlement, it had provided most of the commercial facilities required by both the North and South Pine areas, but the discovery of gold at Gympie in 1867 caused an increase in the number of travellers passing through the region, and this provided the impetus for some limited development.

In the 1870s, the Strathpine region was a sugar-growing area with at least three sugar mills in the vicinity. In the late 1870s, our ancestors Alice White and Abel Pointon were married at Bunya, in upper Strathpine.

One of the first bakeries in the Strathpine area was built in 1882 by Richard Piggott who, with his wife Ellen and other members of their family, operated the bakery and later a store until the business closed down in 1961. In 1895, the post office, which had operated from the Strathpine railway station, was transferred about 400m to and general store on Gympie Road.

South Burnett Region

This Local Government Area was created in March 2008 as a result of the report of the Local Government Reform Commission released in July 2007. Prior to the 2008 amalgamation, the South Burnett Region, located in the southern catchment of the Burnett River, existed as four distinct local government areas:

- the Shire of Kingaroy
- the Shire of Nanango
- the Shire of Murgon
- and the Shire of Wondai.

Nanango

Nanango, a rural town, is 150km north-west of central Brisbane. It was named after the Nanango pastoral run (c.1842) and is one of Queensland's oldest towns. It is believed that the name of the run was derived from an aboriginal word ascribed to a tribal elder or referred to a waterhole.

The original inhabitants of the area were the Aboriginal people belonging to the Wakka Wake (or Wakawaka) people. The area was used as a gateway to the bunya nut festivals, where aboriginals would travel from as far away as the Clarence River in northern NSW and the Maranoa River to feast on bunya nuts.

The area around Nanango was first settled by Europeans in 1847 by John Borthwick and William Oliver from Ipswich taking up pastures for sheep farming. Oliver selected an area of more than

500km² that comprised the blocks of Coolabunia, Booie, Broadwater and Nanango.

The first commercial establishment at the present site of Nanango township was Goode's Inn, founded by prospector Jacob Goode in July 1848. The inn served travellers journeying from Brisbane and Limestone (now known as Ipswich) and became the meeting place for early residents of Taromeo, Tarong and Nanango stations. The town of Nanango quickly developed around it.

In 1850, William Oliver built a red cedar dwelling to which he later added a stone store, stables and blacksmith's shop. Goode's Inn post office opened in January 1852. It was renamed Burnett Inn by 1855 and Nanango on 1 July 1859. In 1861, the town was officially surveyed. The first lots were sold in 1862. In 1866 a school was opened.

Beef, dairy and timber (in particular the valuable red cedar) were the primary early industries in the area. The discovery of gold at the Seven Mile Diggings near Nanango in 1867 precipitated a gold rush, and consequently a population boom. However, the gold deposits were meagre. At one time the population included 700 miners, many of whom were Chinese.

Land in Nanango was open for selection on 17 April 1877: 48 square miles (120km²) were available. As a result, farm selections were taken up. This was part of a closer settlement pattern of the district.

A second population boom occurred when the Brisbane Valley railway line was extended to Yarraman in 1911. Nanango became the terminus of a branch off the South Burnett railway line at Kingaroy on 13 November 1911.

In 1842, Queensland was opened to free settlement and, within a few months, three famous properties were claimed in the region.

Taromeo was 200m² (518km²) and was taken up by Simon Scott, who used it to raise sheep.

My great grandfather, Archibald Lee, first moved to Nanango in 1872 when he took up the role of police magistrate, and over the next 20 years he bought several areas of land around Nanango. Many of his children remained in the area.

A major change in the area came in the early 1900s when much of the land held by the early pastoralists was resumed and subdivided for more intensive agricultural development. Today, the town is a typical rural service centre supporting local industries which include beef and pork production, dairying and milk processing, timber, small crops, grapes and olives.

In about 1938, my grandfather, Frederick Lee, returned to Nanango with his family to live at his farm, Acacia Ridge, now on Lee and Robin Road. The farm is still owned by his grandson, Greg Lee.

The name 'Lee' appears regularly around Nanango, for example: Lee Court, Lee Park Racetrack, Lee Place and Lees Bridge.

Kingaroy

The origin of the name 'Kingaroy' is usually claimed to be derived from the Wakka Wakka aboriginal word for 'red ant'. The Kingaroy rugby league team is known as 'the Red Ants' and a red ant features on the old Kingaroy shire coat of arms.

Rural settlement of the area dates back to 1843, when one of the first selections was made at Burrandowan (west of Kingaroy) by squatter and explorer Henry Stuart Russell. Even though Russell was reputedly the first European to realise the potential of South Burnett, it was Simon Scott of Taromeo (now Blackbutt) and the Haly brothers of Taabinga who brought the first flocks of sheep to the area in the late 1850s.

In 1878, the district where Kingaroy now stands was settled by the Markwell brothers. When the first resumptions were made from the enormous Taabinga holding, the brothers selected two adjoining areas and, in 1883, these leases were converted to freehold and became known as the 'Kingaroy Paddock'. The corner of this paddock was on what is now known as Haly Street, named after the brothers who settled at Taabinga Station about 12km (seven miles) south-west of present-day Kingaroy.

My great grandfather, Abel Pointon, took up Gordon Brook, also part of the former Taabinga holding, in 1888. The Pointon Farm of Gordon Brook was near the Tabbing current Gordonbrook, north-west of Kingaroy[2]. There is still a Pointons Road at Gordonbrook.

Gordonbrook today mainly consists of grazing land, with irrigated crops growing close to the banks of the Stuart River. In 1941, Gordonbrook dam was built to provide Kingaroy and its former WWII airforce base, RAAF Kingaroy, with a reliable water supply.

A small, prosperous village grew up around Taabinga in the 1890s, but the arrival of the railway in 1904 led to a land explosion around Kingaroy and the development of Kingaroy to how it is now. Taabinga quickly declined into a ghost town by the end of World War I, and today the original Taabinga Homestead and a few outbuildings are all that remain. The area opposite Kingaroy airport is today known as 'Taabinga Village', but is really only a suburb of Kingaroy.

Some of Abel Pointon's children were involved in properties in and around Kingaroy, including Manumbar Station and Wywurry. Others went further afield to Gympie and Dalby.

---

[2] 'Gordonbrook' is the term generally used for the current area. However, in the time of Abel Pointon, the farm was known as 'Gordon Brook'.

Wywurry Homestead[iii]

Shire of Kilcoy

Kilcoy was the heartland of the Jinibara people and the name comes from a patch of lawyer cane (a climbing palm endemic in Queensland) on Mt Kilcoy: 'bara' means 'people' or 'folk', thus Jinibara is 'people of the lawyer cane'. Kilcoy was known as Bumgur, meaning the 'blue cod'.

The locality was originally called 'Hopetoun' after early settler Captain Louis Hope. In 1841, brothers Evan and Colin Mackenzie, from the town of Kilcoy in Scotland, took up land west of Durundur (in the Stanley River valley) and began grazing sheep soon after land was opened to free settlement. They renamed it after their home town.

In 1842 on the outskirts of Kilcoy Station owned by MacKenzie, 30-60 aborigines died, believed to be from eating flour that settlers had laced with strychnine or arsenic. However, a thesis by Gerry Langevad in 1980 found that although evidence points to the fact that some such incident did occur, it is insufficient to establish whether it was by accident or design.[3]

The Pointon family farm, 'Hill Farm', established in about 1863, was located just to the east of Kilcoy at Woodford.

In 1864 Captain Hope became sole owner and built the Kilcoy Station homestead of bricks, made on the property, and red cedar. He stayed on in Kilcoy until 1900.

In 1878 brothers Abel and Charles Pointon combined to buy Hereford Hills, at Hopetoun.

Towards the end of the 1800s large properties and Government leases began to be divided up for closer settlement. Blocks capable of supporting a family were eagerly sought after, fenced and cleared. The main source of income for these settlers was dairying.

The site of the town of Kilcoy was surveyed by WE Hill by April 1888, and the first land sale was on 6 November that year. The township, unofficially referred to as 'Hopetoun', quickly developed at the junction of Sheep Station and Kilcoy Creeks to service these settlers and their families. In 1892, a post office was opened. In 1908 the post office name was changed to Kilcoy, to avoid incorrect mail distribution to other towns of the same name in Victoria and Western Australia.

---

[3] Langevad, Gerry (1980) *The Kilcoy massacre : an ethnohistorical exercise*, University of Queensland.

Links to those who travelled to Australia

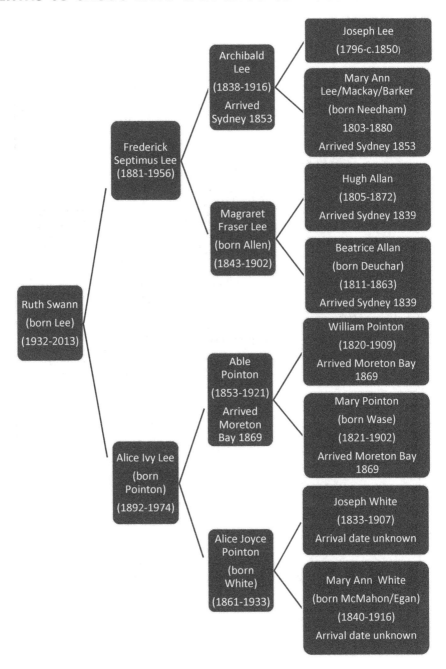

Our British ancestors

The Needham family

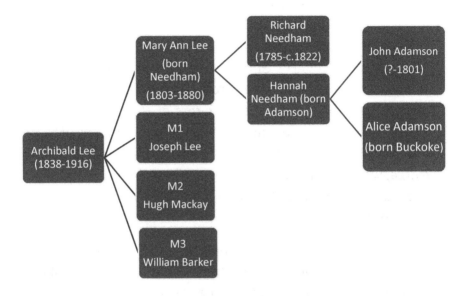

Our connection to the Needham family began with my great, great grandmother, Mary Ann Needham, who married the 19th century linen draper, Joseph Lee.

The Needham name stems back to the Anglo-Saxon tribes of Britain. It is a product of when the family lived in places called 'Needham' in the counties of Derbyshire, Norfolk and Suffolk. In 1547, the manor of Alvaston in the parish of St Michael, Derby, was granted to the Needham family, from whom it passed through various hands.

There was a Thomas Needham born at Needham, Derbyshire, in about 1308, and he was still living there in 1337. He had two known children: Thomas, who was living in 1353, and married Maud Melure (the daughter of Roger Melure of Thornsett, Derbyshire); and William, born about 1330 at Needham,

Derbyshire, who married Alice Cranage. Thomas Needham was of Needham Grange, Derbyshire – the family home.

The family can be traced back several more generations, but with very few details, to a William Needham, who was of Needham, Derbyshire, and Lord of Staunton. He was living in 1102. The Derbyshire branch of the family remained in possession of Thornsett and Needham as rich yeomen until early in the 16th century. Six generations down from Thomas, Otwell Needham married Elizabeth, daughter and heiress of Nicholas Cadman of Cowley. They had 10 sons and five daughters and from six of those sons, many of today's Needhams probably descend. One son, George, went to London and it is possible that our Needham line descends from him, but I have been unable to definitively establish this.

Emigration of Needhams to Australia followed the 'first fleets' of convicts, tradespeople and early settlers, but it is unknown if any of these people can be linked to our ancestors.

Needham settlers in Australia in the 19th century included:

- Frederick Needham, an English convict from Leicester, who was transported aboard the Albion on 21 September 1826, settling in New South Wales
- Emma Needham, who arrived in Adelaide, Australia aboard the ship *Harpley* in 1848
- Isaac Needham, aged 29, who arrived in Adelaide, Australia aboard the ship *Marion* in 1849
- Martha Needham, aged 34, who arrived in Adelaide, Australia aboard the ship *Marion* in 1849.

Richard Needham (c. 1780-before 1823)

This is the first Needham family member I can definitively claim as our ancestor, as he is named in several documents relating to his daughter. However, pinning down the correct Richard Needham was difficult, because there are at least four Richard Needhams born in London around the 1780s that might be ours.

Similarly, tracking down details of his life has been difficult. There are a surprising number of Old Bailey records which mention a Richard Needham, but whether he is ours or not is unknown. For example:

- On 11 April 1804 in the trial of Thomas Daman, who was accused of stealing hay from his employer, Richard Needham (a brewer) gave evidence as the unknowing purchaser of the stolen goods.
- In 1814 there is a record of discharge of Richard Needham from Fleet Prison where he had served time as a debtor.
- In January 1824 there is another record of discharge from Marshalsea Prison, however I am reasonably sure that our Richard had died by this time.
- In April 1824, in the trial of Mary Kelly who was accused of stealing a box, a flat-iron, a half-crown, a shilling and a sixpence, a Richard Needham (headborough – a chief of a frankpledge or tithing) gave evidence. However, again I am reasonably sure that our Richard was dead by this time.

We do know that Richard married 'Hannah', and many family trees I accessed have her listed as Hannah Clayton. However, Hannah Clayton is more often connected to a Thomas Needham who is erroneously listed by a number of family tree researchers as Mary Ann's father, and this is definitely incorrect. Our Hannah was in fact Hannah Adamson from East Barnet, and she married Richard Needham before 1800 because she is already listed as 'Hannah Needham' in her father's will which was written in 1800.

Richard died before 1823 (and after 1805) because Hannah was listed as a widow on her daughter Mary Ann's banns in 1823.

Jenny Kroonstuiver

I am reasonably sure that Richard and Hannah had at least two children:

- **Mary Ann Needham** (1803-1880): our ancestor, (see below)
- **John Needham** (1805-1848): There is a christening record from 25 September 1805 at Friar Street, Blackfriars. He married Eliza Scarlet Lainson and they had four daughters: Clara Emma; Sarah Elizabeth; Mary Webster; Victoria Eliza; and lived in Middlesex. His father had died by the time he married.

This document is the banns announcement for John Needham and Eliza Lainson

John Needham's marriage record from 4 May 1834 St James, Piccadilly (St James, Westminster), London.

I tried to find John Needham on the 1841 census but cannot identify him.

Hannah was still alive in 1841 because she is listed on the census as part of Joseph and her daughter Mary Ann Lee's household, aged 60. There is no sign of her in the 1851 census. There is a death record for a Hannah Needham from October 1845 in Clerkenwell London, which may have been her, but there is insufficient information to verify this as our Hannah.

Mary Ann Needham (1803-1869)

Mary Ann Needham, my fascinating great, great grandmother, was born on 6 November 1803 at Friar Street, Blackfriars, New Jerusalemite, London, England to parents Richard and Hannah Needham. She was most likely baptized on 7 December 1803 at All Hallows, Tottenham, Haringey, Middlesex.

Interestingly, her baptism information lists her denomination as 'Swedenborgian', which was 'new church', and one of several historically related Christian denominations that developed as a new religious group, influenced by the writings of scientist and Swedish Lutheran theologian Emanuel Swedenborg (1688-1772). Also known as the 'New Jerusalem Church', it was established in London in the 1780s, with one prominent follower being the poet William Blake. According to Swedenborg, he received a new revelation from Christ in visions he experienced over a period of at least 25 years. He predicted in his writings that God would replace the traditional Christian Church, establishing a new church that would worship Jesus Christ as God. According to new church doctrine, each person must cooperate in repentance, reformation and regeneration.

Religious alliances were evidently reasonably flexible, but because in August 1823, at the age of 17, Mary Ann Needham married linen draper Joseph Lee at All Hallows Staining, London, a Church of England house of worship. The consent was given by Hannah Needham, widow, so her father had died by this time.

MARRIAGES solemnized, in the Parish of *Allhallows, Staining*
in the County of *London* in the Year 18*33*

Joseph Lee of *the* Parish
of Hornsey in the County of Middlesex Bachelor
and *Mary Ann Needham* of *this* Parish
Spinster a Minor
were married in this *Church* by *Licence* with Consent of
[illegible] this first Day of
August in the Year One thousand eight hundred and *thirty three*
By me *John Roberts [illegible]*
This Marriage was solemnized between us {
In the Presence of {
No. 16.

Record of marriage Mary Ann Needham and Joseph Lee.

When my mother was researching Mary Ann, she contacted a distant cousin in London who sent a list of possible children of Joseph and Mary Ann. Most of this list cross-references with birth records I have since found, except for twins Louisa and Amelia, who were baptised at Lambeth in 1827, and Mary Ann Eliza born in 1850. The year 1827 seems to be the same year that a son, Joseph, was born, so I suspect that the twins were not children of our Joseph and Mary Ann. Also, our Mary Ann would have been 47 when Mary Ann Eliza was born in 1850 and this seems unlikely, especially as Joseph may have died by this time.

So, my list of their children is as follows, and the lives of these children are discussed in the Lee chapter.

- 1826, Mary Ann Lee St. Andrew, Holborn, Middlesex
- 1827, Joseph Lee, St. Marys, Islington, London
- 1828, John Lee
- 1836, Samuel Lee, St. Andrew, Holborn, Middlesex
- 1837, Eliza Ann Lee
- 1838, Archibald Lee, 41 Upper Street, St. Andrew, Holborn, Middlesex (our ancestor)

- 1840, Eliza Charlotte Deuchar (born Lee)
- 1842, Washington Lee, London.

The Lee family appears in the 1841 census. Joseph was a draper at St Andrew, Holborn (above the bars); aged 45; Mary Ann was 35; daughter Mary Ann was 15; son Samuel was 5; Archibald was 3; Eliza was 1. Joseph and John may well have been apprenticed by this time.

By the 1851 census, Mary Ann was a widow, aged 48. She appears in the census as 'house proprietor' living in Church Street, Hackney and the only child living with her was Eliza, aged 11. Interestingly, though, one of her two lodgers was Hugh Mackay (51), a banker's clerk born in Scotland, and the other was his son Daniel aged 16, also a banker's clerk, born in Liverpool, Lancashire. Mary Ann married Hugh MacKay the following year, a few months before they left to travel to Australia.

I have been unable to track down Daniel's mother, nor any record of a first marriage for Hugh Mackay. Hugh is shown as a 'bachelor' and not a 'widower' on his marriage certificate to Mary Ann, so he and Daniel's mother probably never married. Daniel remained in England and, in 1869, aged 28, it is likely that he married Janet Wells at Everton in Lancaster. By this time, he was a police officer, and his father Hugh's profession was listed as 'farmer'. I cannot find him on any census lists after that.

Daniel MacKay's marriage record

At aged 49, Mary Ann married Hugh Mackay, recorded as a 'gentleman', in West Hackney. The fact that his father was listed as a military officer opens up some interesting possibilities for Hugh's earlier life. There is a record for a Hugh MacKay as a member of the 92nd Highlanders from 1835-1836, and then two court martial records (which I cannot access) from 1838 and 1839 in Edinburgh, so it is possible that he commenced a military career like his father. However, there are also various entries for a Hugh MacKay in the Liverpool electoral registers for the 1830s, so he may have been living in Liverpool as a shopkeeper. There is no record of him in the 1841 census.

Hugh MacKay and Mary Ann Lee – marriage licence application

Hugh MacKay and Mary Ann Lee – record of marriage

One of the family tree owners I contacted said that Mary Ann, Hugh, as well as Eliza and Archibald Lee, came to Australia in October 1852, but I have not been able to find them on any passenger lists.

When they arrived, Sydney was in the grip of gold fever as goldfields around Mudgee, Louisa Creek, Orange, Sofala and Hill End, to name a few, were prospering. Stories of bushrangers and daring robberies abounded. Thousands of Chinese miners were arriving with many Sydneysiders openly hostile to these migrants, expressing fears of the possibility of disease and smallpox.

The next reference, after their arrival in Sydney, is a newspaper notice in January 1853 where a wanted advertisement for an engineer and two butchers for the country advised applications were to be made to H. Mackay at 9 Church Street. Later that month another notice advised that a John Taylor had sold his business of the same address to Hugh MacKay, although the nature of the business is not stated. A month later there is a notice about wine sales from the same address (Church Hill, which I think may now be York Street in Sydney), so it can be assumed that this was a in part a merchandising business in partnership with the Lochinvar Vineyard at Maitland. This may the connection with the Aberdeen Company that later led to Archibald Lee heading to Glengallan. I strongly suspect that Hugh Mackay may have had a business relationship with the company, because for several years he advertised for staff etc for both the Darling Downs and the Hunter Valley, and in 1856 jointly advertised the sale of fine woolled ewes with John Deuchar, then of Rosenthal Station. He was also advertised as being able to accept stock bookings for the Warrell Steaming establishment in 1856.

It was evidently a versatile business, because in August 1853, Hugh was advertising for four-five single men as shepherds for the Darling Downs. A month later he advertised for letting a large cottage off the Newtown Road with verandah and eight rooms for possession 'in a few weeks'. In November he was advertising for shepherds again, this time for the Moreton Bay District. In 1854 he advertised Moreton Bay tallow for sale, as well as the A1 ship *Baltasara* for freight or charter. Sometime during 1854, the business moved from No 9 to No 1 Church Hill. In 1855 he was elected to the Sydney Chamber of Commerce.

In 1856 Hugh Mackay was elected as an auditor to the Sydney Exchange Company, and was a member of the organising committee for the Exchange Ball in 1857.

Hugh and Mary Ann were living at a home known as Observatory Villa in Upper Paddington. The Sydney Observatory was built at Millar's Point from 1857-1959.

Hugh Mackay died in September 1858 in London, soon after arriving at the home of his niece.

Mary Ann was a widow for just four years, though, because in May 1872, aged 69, she married for a third time, this time to William Barker, of Melbourne.

MARRIAGES.

BARKER—MACKAY—May 22, at Ophir Cottage, Campbell-street, Newtown, by the Rev. George Sheppard, William Barker, Esq., of Melbourne, to Mary Anne, relict of Hugh Mackay, Esq., formerly of Sydney.

William Barker and Mary Ann MacKay – marriage notice

She died at Manly, at the residence of her daughter Eliza, on 23 May 1880 aged 73.

THE FRIENDS of the late Mrs. MARY A. BARKER are respectfully invited to attend her Funeral; to move from the Circular Quay, THIS Tuesday AFTERNOON, at a quarter to 2 o'clock, to Necropolis. C. KINSELA and SONS, George-street, opposite Christ Church; and Oxford-street, near Crown-street.

Death notice for Mary Ann Barker

Elizabeth Merac and Mary Adamson

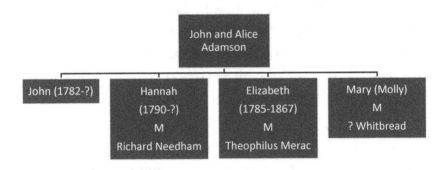

Following Mary Ann's death, there were several letters from her son Archibald to London solicitor John Grey as well as Jacques and Sons, Solicitors in Bristol, seeking to claim inheritances he was entitled to as a result of his mother's death. The Bristol solicitors were handling the will of 'Great Aunt Eliza Merac' from whom he expected a 1/6 share amounting to about £333, while John Grey was handling the will of 'my Great Aunt Mary Ann Adamson' from whom he expected a quarter share amounting to about £275, plus interest. I assume that the quarter share was to be from equal shares to his surviving siblings Samuel, Eliza, Mary Ann, and himself.

Trying to place these two ladies somewhere in the family tree, either as Aunts of Mary Ann or her first husband Joseph, took months. There is a note at the front of Archibald Lee's diaries that "Grandfather's brothers Samuel and Joseph died on the Estate in Southern England, near Bristol, also sisters in England". So, there was a Bristol connection to explore as well.

Both Great Aunts shared the name 'Adamson', which suggested to me that Mary Ann Needham/Lee/Mackay/Barker's mother Hannah Needham may have been an Adamson. This would make the two testators 'great aunts' of Archibald Lee.

With the assistance of a genealogist from England, my theory was eventually confirmed. We located an extraordinarily lengthy and detailed hand-written will written by John Adamson in 1800 – it took days to translate! The will has pages and pages of details regarding the disbursement of annuities to his wife Alice, son John, and daughters Elizabeth (who was still unmarried at the time), Hannah Needham and Molly Whitbread.

John Adamson came from East Barnet, which is an area of north London within the London Borough of Barnet. It is a largely residential suburb whose central area contains shops, public houses, restaurants and services, and the parish church of St Mary the Virgin. The records from this church have been critical in tracking down the Adamson family.

*Google Earth image of St Mary the Virgin Church
in East Barnet*

Despite the evident wealth of John Adamson (the father), there are very few records of him or his children, and they have not been picked up by any other family trees. I am reasonably sure that he married Alice Buckoke in April 1775 at nearby Shenley, Hertford, and there is an 1822 burial record for Alice Adamson at St Mary the Virgin, the East Barnet parish church. There is a burial record from the same church for John Adamson, 'late respectable publican in this parish', for December 1801. While the date fits for our John, I'm not sure that 'publican' does. The John Adamson in this record was the publican of the King's Head, which is still standing, but is now a veterinary practice.

Unfortunately, the baptismal records from St Mary the Virgin have not yet been placed online, although they are tantalisingly available, impeded only by current events. The Hertfordshire Archives, who house the records, ceased being able to take overseas orders due to a post-Brexit restructure of their finance system, and were then closed for months due to the COVID-19 pandemic. There is a standing order for the records when they are able to process it!

Shenley, where John and Alice married, is a village and civil parish in Hertfordshire, England, between Barnet and St Albans. The village is located 18.7 miles from Central London.

I believe that son John was a furniture maker, as I found evidence in the *Dictionary of English Furniture Makers* of an indenture to a Samuel Burton in 1793, and John was admitted freeman of the Upholder's Co in 1803. The term 'Upholder' is an archaic word for 'upholsterer'. In past times Upholders carried out not just the manufacture and sale of upholstered goods but were cabinet makers, undertakers, soft furnishers, auctioneers and valuers. John Adamson was listed as operating at 63 Fenchurch Street, London, which was also the location of a Robert Adamson, a joinery and mahogany turner in the 1750s whose trade card stated that he 'Makes all sorts of Cabinet Looking Glasses and Mahogany Goods at the lowest Prices. NB. Funerals perform'd & Goods Appraised'. This suggests that furniture making was a family business, and it is possible that Robert was an uncle of John who was also listed as a Carpenter from Chiswick, aged 36, in a Masons register. In later directories, John was listed as an Auctioneer from 58 Fenchurch Street (and was still there 1823 – in *Kent's Original London Directory*).

Mary Adamson

In searching for Mary Adamson, I had to consider that she might have been either born Adamson, or married John Adamson. After finding John's father's will there are two possibilities: she married John; or she is the daughter Molly listed in the will. This is possible, because 'Molly' was frequently a pet name for 'Mary', but she was married 'Whitbread' in 1800 at the time of her father's will, and this is not mentioned. Because her solicitors were in London, I assumed that she probably lived there. She had another solicitor in Kent, so I expanded the search to there as well. However, the trail mostly ran cold.

I also found a notice of probate for Mary Sophia Adamson who had lived in Islington and who had died on 2 December 1880. This was proved by her brother John Skrymsher. While the address seems about right, the personal estate was under £100, which is well under Archibald's expectations, and his letters are dated July 1880 which is before her death, so this one is out! No other probate notice seems to fit.

Eliza Merac

I eventually had more luck identifying Elizabeth Merac.

Archibald Lee's 'great aunt Eliza' was born Elizabeth Adamson in East Barnet, Middlesex, c.1785. She married Theophilus Merac, his third marriage, in 1826.

The Merac family, of French origin and possibly Jewish, had been operating in London at least since 1761, because I found a record for Moses Merac, an apprentice haberdasher with 'Rich Whitten'. His wife's name was Mary and he died at Pentonville in 1812. I am assuming that this Moses was the father of the brothers Theophilus (b. 1771) and Moses Laporte (b. 1774) Merac, two wealthy merchants based in Queen Street, Cheapside.

The Merac brothers were business partners, and there is quite a bit of documentary evidence about them.

In 1795, Merac T & Co are listed as merchants, 6 Love-lane Aldermanbury.

- In 1796 Theophilus paid land tax records at Cripplegate Within, London.

- In 1801 Theophilus was living at 18 Park Street. Theophilus owned several properties along Park Street and these were listed for sale in 1835.

- In 1802 Theophilus married Laurentia Ann Fellow at Saint Antholin, Budge Row, London, however she died in Bristol (Clifton) in 1805. There is no record of any children.

- In September 1803, there is an Old Bailey record where Thomas Wright and Lancelot Hoggart were tried for stealing muslin shawls, cambric, gingham, waistcoats and gauze, "the property of Moses Laporte Merac and Theophilus Merac, in their dwelling house." The prisoners were acquitted.

- In 1805 Moses Laporte Merac married Elizabeth Manning.

- Elizabeth and Moses had five children – (there are records for all of these):

  o Robert Manning Merac 20 Aug 1806
  o Elizabeth Ann Merac 11 Sept 1807
  o Mary Ann Merac 9 July 1811
  o Theophilus Merac 11 Feb 1818
  o Sarah Augusta Merac 30 May 1838 (which seems a bit odd as the date is 20 years after previous baby, so is more likely a grandchild, even though the parents are cited as Moses and Elizabeth Ann).

- In 1807 Theophilus and Moses were declared bankrupt and there is a newspaper notice advertising the sale of Theophilus' household effects including *"handsome 4-post bedsteads with rich chintz hangings, window curtains to correspond, excellent feather beds and bedding, elegant drawing room suite etc ...."* In addition the lease of the premises was also sold comprising *"an excellent dwelling house, with coach-house, stable, yard, garden and stack of warehouses…".* Their Certificate (of discharge) was granted soon afterwards.

- The last dividends were paid out in April 1808, and soon after that they were back at Guildhall, as well as being back and operating again at Queens Street.

The Guildhall connection*: Guilds composed of workmen from specific trades and crafts were established in the middle ages. Their purpose was to defend the interests of the trade, regulate the quality of workmanship and the training of new members, and provide support and welfare for their members. Established by charter and regulated by the City of London, London's guilds also provided a political voice to their members, whom as freemen of the City, had the right to elect members of the Court of Aldermen and Common Council. London had eighty-nine guilds in the eighteenth century, ranked according to a hierarchy of precedence with the twelve Great Companies at the top. The powers of the guilds to regulate economic activity declined substantially in the 18th century, and their primary functions were increasingly confined to providing social prestige, business contacts and a political voice to their members. They also provided substantial charity to their members, partly funded by large charitable bequests which they administered.*

Source: https://www.londonlives.org/static/Guilds.jsp

- In 1809 Theophilus married Ann Sarah Howard, his second marriage. There is no record of any children.
- 1820: Theophilus' second wife, Anne Sarah, died.

- 1821: Theophilus is listed as a member of the United Grand Lodge of England Freemasons, mariners Lodge Bristol. His profession is listed as 'Accomptant', which is an accountant.
- 18 March 1826: Theophilus married again, for a third time, to Elizabeth Adamson in Bristol. There is no record of them having any children.

Theophilus Merac and Elizabeth Adamson, marriage record.

- In 1838, there is a record of an annual subscription to the British Association for the Advancement of Science, from Theophilus Merac of College Green, Bristol. Theophilus is also listed as a resident of 18 College Green in the *Bristol and Clifton Directory and Alamack* of 1851, included in the 'General list of names of the gentry, merchants, Professors and Tradesmen of Bristol". This is the first time we have an address for a possible 'family estate' in Bristol.
- 1841 – Moses died aged 66.
- 1841 census – Elizabeth (58) and Theophilus (70) were living at St Clement Danes and there were three servants, so it is clear that they retained their London residence as well as the one in Bristol.

- 1851 – Theophilus died at 18 College Green, Bristol.
- 1851 census – Elizabeth (Moses' wife) was listed as a widow, living in Brunswick Sq, Shoreditch. Her occupation was listed as 'annuitant' which is a person who receives an annuity. Her unmarried daughter Elizabeth aged 39 (she died 1891) was also living there.
- 1861 census – Elizabeth (Theophilus' wife) was recorded as a widow aged 75, living with servant Elizabeth Hunt at 18 College Green, Bristol.

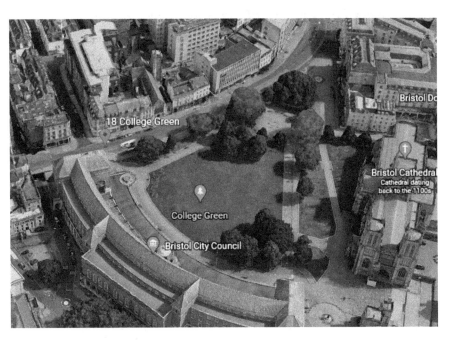

Googe Earth image of the College Green residence

The name 'College Green' also applied to the road which passed on all three sides of the triangular Green. From 1869, the southern leg of this formed part of the new Deanery Road, being the main route out of Bristol heading to the south-west and separating the Green from the Cathedral, whilst the northern leg (from 1758) led down to a crossroads with Frog Lane and Frogmore Street and up Park Street towards Clifton. In 1851 a replica of the High Cross was erected and placed at the apex of the Green. This remained here until a statue of Queen Victoria (by Joseph Boehm) took its place in 1888, at which time the replica Cross was moved to the centre of the Green, at the intersection of the formal promenades where the original had stood between 1736 and 1762. For the next sixty years the Green remained a leafy oasis, insulated from the busy roads on either side by a double row of tall trees, though slightly diminished by the removal of the outer row of trees on the south side around 1885 and on the north side for road-widening in 1926.

- Elizabeth died at the College Green house on 28 February 1867 and Mary Ann Mackay (Archibald Lee's mother) was named as an executor alongside Thomas Wilson Hall (he was cashier from the Old Bank). Mary Ann had already married William Barker by this time, but I doubt the Bristol solicitors knew about this or that Elizabeth's will had been altered accordingly. The probate record valued her estate as 'Effects under £5000'. Elizabeth's probate valuation of £5,000 is equivalent to over £500,000 in today's money.

Elizabeth Merac, death record

Given the fact that Mary Ann was evidently very close to her Aunt Elizabeth, and was named an executor, I think it is safe to assume that the Bristol address was the 'estate' Archibald was referring to in relation to the deaths of his brothers Joseph and Samuel, although there is no documentary evidence to substantiate this.

The Lee family

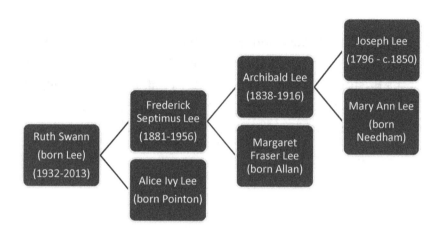

Joseph Lee (1796-before 1851)

Our earliest known Lee ancestor is Joseph Lee, a linen draper in London in the early 1800s. There were more than 150 such drapers in the greater London area at the time, with Joseph's establishment listed as being at 41 Liverpool Road, Islington. At that time, Islington was a site of new housing developments for the 'comfortably well off'. The Angel Inn had been long established – the inn and surrounding area were named after lands belonging to St John's Priory and the building was being used as an inn by the end of the 16th century and known as 'the Angel' by 1614. The inn took its name from the Angel of the Annunciation, which appeared on the sign. By about the 1760s, urban development in the area had begun, with more rapid growth after the 1820s. So, in Joseph's time, he would have been servicing a reasonably well-heeled clientele.

Joseph was a Londoner, having been born in Middlesex (outer London) in about 1796. There is no information about his parentage or early life. It is possible that he was the son of another Joseph Lee, also a linen draper. There is a City Directory entry for a Joseph Lee, linen draper, at 67 Blackman Street, Borough, in 1811, but no way of linking this to our Joseph. There was also a Joseph Lee born to parents Joseph and Sarah Lee at Whitechapel in 1770, but, again, there is no way of verifying that this is the correct parentage. There is an 1803 court record from the Old Bailey for a Joseph Lee, linen draper, where he gave evidence against Sarah Ealey for the theft of handkerchiefs and a cloth wrapper when he was moving from Fore-Street to a house in Chiswell Street. There are also a series of workhouse records, but my impression is that our Lees were reasonably wealthy, so I do not think the ones from the workhouse are our relatives.

Upper St, looking north c.1840.[v]

In 1823, at the age of 27, Joseph married 20-year-old Mary Ann Needham at All Hallows Staining. Mary Ann was supported by her widowed mother, Hannah. It seems that both Mary Ann and Joseph were literate, as they signed their own names. All Hallows Staining was a Church of England house of worship in the north-eastern corner of Langbourn ward in London, close to Fenchurch Street railway station. This old church had survived the Great Fire of London in 1666, but collapsed in 1671. It was thought its foundations had been weakened by too many burials in the churchyard close to the church walls. The church was rebuilt in 1674, and this is the church in which Joseph and Mary Ann were married. All Hallows Staining was demolished in 1870, leaving only the tower.

In 1830, Joseph's shop was quite possibly at 41 Hedge Row, Islington, as there was an entry in the London City Directory 1830 for a Joseph Lee, draper.

Joseph and Mary Ann spent most of their married life at 41 Upper Street, Holborn, a suburb of Islington. This street ran directly parallel to the street where the drapery shop was located. Their dwelling was most likely above a bar, which may still exist today as the Steam Passage Tavern. In the 1841 census, they were listed in the parish of 'St Andrew, Holborn (above the bars)', and we know this was 41 Upper Street from the birth certificates of their children. However, Upper Street has undergone many name and renumbering changes over the centuries, and the location may have been above a different tavern.

The 1841 census entry lists Joseph and Mary Ann, along with children Mary Ann, Samuel, Archibald and Eliza. There is also a 'Hannah Newham' (60), but as the age of this person fits Mary Ann's widowed mother, I suspect this was meant to be Hannah Needham. Mary Adams (16) lived there as well, probably as a servant.

In the early 19th century when Joseph and Mary Ann lived in Upper Street, there were the remains of ancient buildings in the area, the old Vicarage House, the Pied Bull Inn etc., and Islington, particularly in the haymaking season, was still predominantly rural, with occasional strayed cattle and a village green. The spread of building from the 1830s can be attributed to the introduction of omnibuses which allowed clerks and artisans to join merchants and professional men in living farther from their employment. This was really the peak of wealth for Islington, because from the 1850s onwards the poor were moving in and middle-class residents began to move to outer Middlesex. However, most of our branch of the Lee family had moved to Australia by then.

Joseph and Mary Ann had at least eight children: Mary Ann (b 1824); Clara (b 1826); Joseph (1827), John (1828), Samuel (b 1835); Archibald (b 1838), Eliza (b 1840) and Washington (b 1842).

Between 1842 and 1852, Joseph died. This was probably before the 1851 census, because Joseph is not readily identifiable on that census and it is highly likely that Mary Ann was a widow by then.

Mary Ann remarried, to Hugh MacKay, in May 1852 in West Hackney and later that year the couple, with Mary Ann's children Eliza and Archibald, travelled to Sydney, arriving in October 1852.

Below is a summary of what happened to their children.

Mary Ann Lee (1824-1891)

Mary Ann seems to have married William Lee (1827-1896) in Lambeth, London. Their daughter Esther was born in London, but by the 1851 census it seems they were living at Bishops Stortford Hertfordshire (north of London). Their sons William (born 1854) and Robert (born 1957) and daughter Jane (born 1860) were born at Lambeth and they were still there in the 1861 census. Another daughter Ellen (born 1863) and son Walter (born 1865) were born at Lambeth but by the time of the 1881 census William and Mary Ann were alone at Battersea London. Mary Ann died at Wandsworth.

Clara Lee (1826-?)

Clara was born on 28 February 1826 at Islington and was baptised at St. Mary's Church Islington. In West Hackney in March 1850, she married Amidee Francois Rimond, a widower and son of an Inspector of woods and forests in France. It seems that their surname may have been Anglicised to 'Raymond' and she possibly died in Islington in 1864, but it was very difficult to trace this family. It is also possible that she was still alive in 1891, because there is a 'Clara Rayment', aged 65, a widow, listed as a lodging housekeeper at 4 Toldfield Terrace, St Marylebone. Her son, Richard Rayment, aged 40 and a clerk, was also living there.

Joseph Lee (1827-?)

Joseph was baptised on 24 March 1827 at St Mary, Middlesex.

In the 1841 census he was an apprentice linen draper, aged 15, at Tottenham Court Road. On the two census pages there were 38 adults and 13 apprentices, all linen drapers, at the same address. The household head is not shown, so it is a reasonable assumption that he was at a large establishment. There are four similar pages for Tottenham Court Road, so it was a very large business. Listed occupations included porters, apprentices, linen drapers, clerks, shopmen and tailors.

This was most likely Lavell and Chapman, silk merchants and linen drapers, who occupied the premises at 263 Tottenham Court Road from 1836. They called their business premises 'Victoria House' and sold *"a choice and superior assortment of drapery goods, of every description, which, for fashion, variety, and extent, is not usually met with in one establishment"*. The partnership only lasted a few years and, in February 1838, it was dissolved, with Chapman to continue on his own. Chapman's shop was frequently visited by shoplifters and 1840 was a particularly bad year for him. It started in March 1840, with Isaac Eggenton, who stole 22 yards of printed cotton – he was sent to Parkhurst Prison on the Isle of Wight and then to Auckland, New Zealand. There are many records of Chapman's shopmen giving evidence at the Old Bailey. The drapery in Tottenham Court Road only lasted until 1845, when Chapman assigned his estate and effects on to John Bradbury and Henry Sturt, both warehousemen, for the benefit of his creditors.[4]

Along the same street in the 1841 census were a toolmaker, watchmaker, baker, upholsterer, ironmonger, painter, milliner, accountant, surgeon, cab driver, hairdresser, turner, wine merchant, corn dealer, ivory turner, lather filler and butcher. It was certainly an affluent area.

Some family trees suggest that this Joseph came to Australia, but I don't think this is correct, because notes in Archibald Lee's letter book state that both Samuel and Joseph died "on the estate in southern England, near Bristol".

My best guess is that he married 'Susan', although I cannot find any marriage record that actually fits. In the 1851 census Joseph, aged 24, was married to 'Susan', and a 'warehouseman packer', and living at 14 Charles Street, Shoreditch – that is the closest census possibility for that year. He may also have died in Shoreditch in 1867.

John Lee (1828-?)

John was born in Islington and his birth was registered as being of the Wesleyan denomination. However, it was very difficult to trace him after that. There is no record of him on the 1841

---

[4] londonstreetviews.wordpress.com/2017/04/25/george-albert-chapman-linen-draper/ sourced September 2020

census – if he was still alive he would have been 13 and most likely apprenticed by that time.

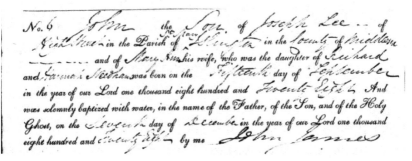

Birth record for John Lee

Samuel Lee (1835-1914)

Samuel was born at 41 Upper Street, the family residence, on January 8, 1835. By the age of 15, 1851, he was an apprentice bookseller living in the household of M Dollman in Hove. There are too many possibilities in the 1861 census to clearly identify him. Similarly, there are several possible marriages, although I favour the marriage in 1870 to Susannah Winkler in Islington. Notes in Archibald Lee's letter book state that Samuel died "on the estate in southern England, near Bristol", but I have been unable to find any likely death records.

Eliza Ann Lee (1837-1842)

Born in 1837, Eliza was baptised at St Mary's Lambeth in Surry, but died as a child. There is a death record for an Eliza Ann Lee, aged 5, at St Mary's Islington in 1842. However, this is after the birth of Eliza Charlotte Lee (see below), which does seem a bit odd. It was not unusual to reuse the name of a deceased child, but to repeat the name of a living child is quite unusual, so this may not have been the correct death record.

Archibald Lee (1838-1916)

Archibald is our ancestor and is discussed below.

Eliza Charlotte Deuchar (born Lee) (1840-1923)

The family was at Upper Street when Eliza was born in 1840, as the following baptism record shows.

Eliza Charlotte Lee – baptism record

Eliza probably came to Sydney with mother and stepfather Hugh MacKay, and perhaps under his name, in October 1852. She would have been aged 12, and it is likely that her brother, Archibald, travelled with them.

She was just 16 when she married Aberdeen Scotsman John Deuchar at the home of her mother and stepfather Hugh MacKay in Paddington, NSW, on August 4, 1857. The ceremony was conducted by a Rev Dr MacKay, who may have been a relative of her stepfather. At the time, John Deuchar was a resident of Rosenthal Station on the Darling Downs, and their story continues in the Deuchar chapter, as the Lee and Deuchar families continued to be intertwined. They had seven children:

- Mary Ann Rattray Gunn (born Deuchar) (1858-1924)
- John Seafield Deuchar (1859-1899)
- George Archibald Deuchar (1861-1890)
- William Glen Deuchar (1864-1931)
- Lindsay Deuchar (1866-1947)
- Allan Deuchar (1867-1947)
- Florence Ada Waugh (born Deuchar) (1870-1905)

Eliza was aged 33 when her husband, John, died. Her second marriage was to William Wilson, manager of the Electric Telegraph Department, Sydney, and he brought one daughter to the marriage – Mrs McGuanne, of Portland.

Eliza died in 1923 in Burwood, Sydney.

Washington Lee (1842-1870)

Washington was left behind when the rest of the family travelled to Australia in 1852. I think he may have been at a boarding school in Hertford, England, because the 1851 census lists him with a long register of other male children of the same age and from various locations. Given that Washington later became a doctor, this was most likely Christ's Hospital at Hertford, which had a long tradition as an endowment school with some dubious traditions. For example, in 1815 an MP named Sir Eyre Coote, entered Christ's Hospital's mathematical school, sent away the younger boys and paid the older ones for a session of mutual flogging. The school nurse arrived to find him buttoning his breeches. England's satirical press had come of age in time to make the most of such a moment. Coote endured a cartoon by George Cruikshank (see below), a vaunted caricaturist, and became a national humiliation.

c.1816 A Peep into the Blue Coat School[vi]

By the 1861 census, Washington was a medical student living at Newington and already married to Frances (Fanny) Stretton and living at a boarding house owned by Fanny's mother. It is likely that they married in October 1860 at St George, Hanover Square, Hyde Park, London.

Six years later, Washington was engaged as a ship's surgeon for the *La Hogue* and travelled to Sydney with his wife as a passenger, arriving in November 1867.

By 1869, he was in Warwick, Queensland, practicing as a doctor, and appointed as a magistrate of the territory in April 1869. No doubt he had been enticed to the area by his sister Eliza, who by then was married to John Deuchar and living at Glengallan Station. He was also appointed as one of the medical doctors to the local hospital and quickly became a respected surgeon. This included providing a service to his own relatives, as this article from 1868 shows:

> ✗ On Wednesday morning last an accident, which was fortunately not attended by any serious consequences, happened to John Deuchar, Esq., of Glengallan station. It appears that he was descending the stairs of his new mansion when he tripped and fell to the bottom. Dr. Lee was at once sent for, who on arrival found that the injuries received were not so serious as at first anticipated ; and we are happy to state that the gentleman is now able to go about as usual. We would not have mentioned the matter were it not that the most alarming rumors were current through the town respecting it.

Warwick Examiner, Sat 11 January 1868

A year later, Washington died from complications most likely caused by a fall from a horse which had rolled on him about six months before his death. He was just 28 when he died and does not appear to have had any children.

His wife, Frances, died in Queensland in 1902.

Archibald Lee (1838-1916)

Our ancestor, Archibald, was 14 when he travelled to Sydney with his mother and stepfather in October 1852. He worked in an office for the three years before going to Brisbane in 1856. After a stay of only a day or two, he rode from Brisbane to the Darling Downs, and spent the next three years gaining experience on Glengallan Station, by then owned by John Deuchar, his brother-in-law.

He evidently quickly became an accomplished horseman and stockman, because in 1860 he went overland to Melbourne in charge of 10,000 wethers. A year later he left the Darling Downs for the Maranoa district west of Roma, found and took up some country on the head of the Amby Creek, the furthest-out occupied run at the time being Bindebango.

In 1862 he took delivery of Wallumbilla Station to the east of Roma, and the following year took the first sheep up to the new country taken up on the Amby, now called Kilmorey. His partner was his sister's brother-in-law, George Deuchar – afterwards a well-known and highly respected figure in the Stanthorpe district. This purchase was tied to the Aberdeen Company, as the Brisbane Courier announced in February 1862 that the station had been sold privately by William Gordon to John Deuchar. The property, which carried 23,000 sheep, was sold for £23,000.

It was while he was at Wallumbilla that he married, in May 1863, Margaret Fraser Allan, his partner George Deuchar's niece, and two of his sons were born at Wallumbilla. He stayed there until 1869. The story of the Allan family (his wife's family) is told in a separate chapter.

We are lucky to have copies of Archibald's letter book from Wallumbilla, carefully typed up by his granddaughter Nancy Carlyon. These letters provide an invaluable insight into the challenges of setting up and running a remote station in the mid-

19th century, as well as Archibald's forthright personality, where he never left anyone in any doubt as to his intentions and meaning. Most of these letters were to the bankers in Sydney, their Ipswich suppliers, the colonial secretary, and Fanning Griffith & Co (merchants and bankers) in Sydney.

Examples of some of the insights they offer appear below.

- **July 1863, to E&W Paul, Sydney:** "We enclose a cheque for £2/2/- is payment of sub to Sydney Mail & Punch, and we are much obliged for your trouble. With reference to our loss by the floods in the early part of the year we found they were not so great as first imagined, and nothing that a good lambing this year will not a great deal more than cover."

- **August 1863, to the Colonial Secretary:** "We would beg to call to your attention the extremely inconvenient way in which our station, Wallumbilla, is situate, consequent upon the late division of the Police districts of Roma and Surat – we are placed in the latter district and the fact of our being at least twice the distance from Surat, than from Roma, together with our being on the main road to the last named township, and as a consequence more in communication with it, appears to have been entirely overlooked...."

- **September 1863, to T&G Harris, suppliers:** "We think four months little enough time for payment of your accounts as the goods are generally six months on the road, and we are never able to approve them before payment."

- **December 1863, to Mort and Co:** "Fifty bales of our this year's clip [sic] are on their way to you, particulars as under. You will please dispose of them to best advantage and forward proceeds to Bank of Australasia, Ipswich."

- **January 1864, to Perry Bros:** "... We have received the plough; it is much too light for our purpose. We regret to be compelled to complain about the quality of many of the things last sent up by you, particularly the shears, we relied upon you to send good ones – but we had a great deal of trouble with our shearers in consequence of their bad quality."

- **April 1864, Bank of Australasia, re an altered cheque:** "... one glance was sufficient to see that the cheque had been tampered with, and we do not intend to suffer for the carelessness and neglect of your clerks – we shall expect you to credit us with the difference."

- **May 1864, to the Surveyor General, re missing application forms:** "We have since learned that the mail with our letter (containing forms) has been robbed so it is doubtful that the application would reach you in time."

- **August 1864, to Wilson & Co:** "We find that our stock of tea is not sufficient until one dray's return, so you will please send up a couple of chests by first opportunity ..."

- **August 1864, to Wilson & Co:** "...we are surprised to hear that carriers are so scarce. We have noticed several small parties of men from Ipswich going up country to their employers, with pack horses and swags, however we are not particularly anxious for our lot as at present there appears every prospect of getting plenty of labour this season ..."

- **September 1864, to the Colonial Treasurer:** payment of £356 for rent and assessment of the following runs: Wallumbilla, Willum Willum, Tenovin, Omidol, Dooladie, Paybah Downs and Fairfield, Byan Byan, Aleurah No 1, Kilmorey, Mecurah and Orallo Nos 1 and 2 – payments from WP Gordon, and Deuchar and Lee

- **October 1864, to Edward Maggarath, Publican:** "The second order drawn by Robt. Bell for £21 we return to you, and are much astonished that you should have the assurance to present such an order, and expect to be paid – after this notice no orders will be paid by us – a very pretty state of things if all our men are to draw orders on us at their pleasure …"

- **November 1864, to the Bank of Australia:** "…we are glad to be able to say, that our clip this year (consistently of about 120-130 bales), is in very satisfactory condition – free from grass seed and clean …"

- **December 1864, to the Commissioner of Police:** "we wrote to you some time ago with reference to a man of the name of Bell who had absconded with two horses, saddles etc, our property, requesting you to insert an advertisement in the *Police Gazette*."

- **January 1865, to Mr Sydney in Dalby:** "We received a letter from you last Monday week, stating that a servant girl had arrived in Dalby, for us from Ipswich, and that you would forward her by coach to Condamine immediately. In consequence of which we sent a man off with horses to Condamine to meet her, who waited the arrival of two mails, but no girl arrived. We have since received a letter from Messrs. Wilson of Ipswich that the girl is still in Dalby …"

- **One week later:** "… with regard to Mary McIntosh, who unfortunately has turned out badly – it appears she never went near Mr Sydney at all as you instructed her to do, we have directed Mr Sydney to summons her, not with any idea of securing her services, but to cancel the agreement and make her pay expenses …"

- **January 1865, GH Wilson, Ipswich:** "The horse dray with Mr Powell and married couple arrived safely, we like the dray etc, but think the price high for the horse. Now we see it we have bought quite as good looking a horse up here for £20. Although we admit the one got from you is good of the kind, or he would not have brought the dray up as he did …"

- **January 1865 to J Moorehead:** "I beg to inform you that a man named Stephen Redcliffe, (late from Bendemeer and Cumkillenbar) died here yesterday morning and was buried this morning – he had been lying on the road between this and Bendemeer for some days, unable to move and very weak from dysentery, and I caused him to be brought on here where he only lived for about 1 ½ days."

- **March 1866 to Fanning Griffith & Co:** "… we have no idea of disposal of surplus stock this season, preferring to stock up our vacant country with the increase …"

- **May 1866 to Fanning Griffith & Co:** "We are glad to be able to say that all sheep are in good condition with scarcely any decrease since the commencement of weaning … on the whole we think you will find that our average expenditure for each month does not much exceed £300. … With reference to the carrying capability of our runs we are in possession of no official documents that would give us any information on this point – a block of 25 square miles is estimated to carry 6,000 sheep, we believe by Government estimate, but near as possible we consider that Wallumbilla would carry from 25 to 30,000 sheep in average season besides cattle, and if seasons could be depended on, we think 40,000 is under its capability …"

- **August 1866 to Fanning Griffith & Co:** "Our clip this year will be 170-180 bales of about an average of 380 or 400 lbs. This wool will be hand washed."

- **October 1866, to the Chief Commissioner of Crown Lands, after several terse exchanges:** "… The simple state of the case is this, that we understand from late surveys that there is not *nearly enough* country on the *Wallumbilla Creek* to represent what we *have been,* and *are,* paying for, and we wish to be informed by you *what* blocks are thrown out?"

- **November 1866 to Fanning Griffith & Co**: "... We are about starting 9,000 weaners to Glengallan to be shorn, and this will be much to our advantage as the wool will be spout washed and much earlier in the market ... We should much prefer you disposing all of our clip in Sydney this year, the market seems to be improving there very much ..."

In February 1866, Wallumbilla was briefly caught up in a failed expedition to Coopers Creek in search of the lost German explorer Ludwig Leichardt. The Leichardt party had last been seen on 3 April 1848 at Allan Macpherson's station, Cogoon, on the Darling Downs. The 1866 search expedition ended in disaster as many members nearly died from thirst, with one member, a Dr Murray, taken to Wallumbilla by a camel driver after being separated from the rest of the party and left behind.

By the end of 1866, it was becoming clear that debts were mounting, and credit was increasingly being extended by Fanning Griffith & Co. These difficulties were further reflected in Archibald Lee's letters.

- **February 1867 to Fanning Griffith & Co**: "Mr Lee when down in Glengallan had some conversation... with Mr John Deuchar when it was agreed that it would be better to part with one of the stations than going on working under all the disadvantages which our debt to you presents. We were disposed at one time to part with Kilmorey but on secondary consideration we would rather hold it and sell Wallumbilla ..."
- **One week later, to Fanning Griffith & Co, re possibility of selling Wallumbilla**: "... we think it is the best thing for us to do. At the same time, we are now aware that this is an unfavourable season for this purpose, and that we must be content with lower prices... Our best plan is to hold on quietly ready for an advantageous opportunity of sale which

may present itself, in the meantime we will endeavour to dispose of what stock we have for sale ..."

- **March 1867, to Fanning Griffith & Co:** "We have written to Mr Henry Beal placing Wallumbilla on the market with 20,000 sheep which together with cattle stores, horses, etc should make a purchase money of about £20,000."

- **July 1867, to Fanning Griffith & Co:** "...we can only say that it is our fixed intention to sell, but as we have not succeeded in finding a purchaser up to this date it would be much better for us and we should prefer holding until after shearing, with a heavy clip before us and every prospect of a good lambing ..."

- **November 1867, from Archibald to his sister 'Lizzie' Deuchar:** "...with regard to offering one of the stations for sale, we of course, can do so, but doubt that it will be accepted due to the tremendous fall in values which has upset all our early calculations."

The writing is not clear, but it seems that by this time they were trying to meet a debt of about £17,500.

Cash must have been scarce, because in January 1868, Archibald was summoned to Warwick Police Court by Duncan McLaughlan for nearly £28 of wages due, a sum which was reduced by the value of stores supplied to the complainant.

For the next few months, the partners did everything they could to raise funds to repay the debt, at least in part, including offering a smaller station, Fairfield, for sale, for which they had an offer in early June 1868, but by August they still had not heard anything further from the prospective buyer.

- **July 1868, to Fanning Griffith & Co:** "Both Mr George Deuchar and the writer have had it in contemplation for some time to work the two places [Wallumbilla and

> Kilmorey] separately, to in fact dissolve the partnership – we should like to know your opinion …"

They wrote in September 1868 to say they were now in a position to sell a larger draft (of stock) to boil (presumably for tallow) and felt that it would take until June to following year to considerably reduce the debt owed.

Their fortunes continued to decline and, in December, they wrote that the season was dry and they were dismayed at the significant fall in wool prices. They saw the solution as being in fencing, claiming that the cost could be recovered in one season through less shepherds' wages and higher lambing rates.

In March, they wrote saying the poor season had prevented an increase in stock and admitted they did not see any opportunity in reducing the debt by June as promised.

By April, they proposed to sell Kilmorey, the purchase money going to the reduction of the debt, which would leave them in a better position to work out the balance on Wallumbilla.

In May 1869, Fanning Griffith & Co advised that they intended to foreclose on both stations. The partners claimed it had taken them by surprise, as the company had promised to carry them until June and they were still hoping to sell Kilmorey. They did, however, sign the deed that month, undertaking to pay the station liabilities, and with the hope of recovering the stations at some stage. It was at this point that the letters ended. Some years later the properties were sold.

It is worth noting that by 1871, their creditor, Frederick Fanning, owned 22 properties in Queensland, mainly in the Maranoa district, although many of these stations were sold by the 1880s.

In October 1868, Archibald had a brief but disastrous appointment as a returning officer for the election of a member to the legislative assembly at Roma. A scathing article printed in the Daily Herald and Western Queensland Advertiser a few days later accused that "armed with the power of the law, he usurped that power, to the detriment of himself and his would-be member Mr Miles".

After leaving Wallumbilla, the Lee family lived at Warwick for about 18 months, until Archibald was appointed to the criminal prosecution service in September 1871. His only daughter, Ethel, was born at Warwick and, while there in 1870, Archibald was appointed a justice of the peace, along with his brother, Dr Washington Lee.

Archibald entered the government service at Nanango and, in 1872, was appointed police magistrate, after having been appointed clerk of petty sessions in 1871. He remained in Nanango as police magistrate, land commissioner, district registrar of births, deaths and marriages, warden of gold fields, etc, for the next 23 years, until 1895, and was then transferred as police magistrate to Barcaldine.

He was evidently a very popular magistrate and an address signed by 38 Nanango residents (including Abel Pointon) on news of his transfer to Barcaldine, and published in *The Capricornian*, stated:

> *"During the twenty-eight years that you have held office in Nanango, as Police Magistrate, and Land Commissioner, you have won our united respect and esteem, both by your unvarying impartiality and courtesy in matters official, and for your ready help and support in all projects that you considered promoted the best interests of the district."*

The original framed document is still on the wall at the
Acacia Ridge farm at Nanango

Once again, we have access to some of his letters from the
Nanango period. In 1880 he was still ordering goods from Wilson
& Co in Ipswich, the suppliers he had used at Wallumbilla. He was
not averse to complaining, though, as this excerpt from a letter in
1881 shows:

> *"Since writing on the 22nd I have received your account*
> *to the end of year – I object to your charge of 5/- for*
> *engaging Schaler – who is the direct opposite of what*
> *I sent to you for and useless for bush life.*
>
> *I could get men here for about 1/- a week, good*
> *bushmen at 15/- to £1, but preferred a stranger to the*
> *district. The washers at Colinton this year were only*

getting £1 per week – what was Smith to get for bringing him up? After 17 years dealings with you I am sorry it was not worth your while to take a little more trouble with such small matters of importance to me. I should have been glad if you intimated that you could not meet with a suitable person, but you wired you had a good man or I would not have troubled you after Daniells had left."

Most interesting though, was the dispute he had with the Department of Public Instruction in February 1880 over his son's teacher Mr Breen who had evidently failed to recommend Archibald's son for a scholarship. Mr Breen, formerly from Bunya, had been promoted to Nanango as head teacher in 1877. Archibald accused Mr Breen of being supportive and complimentary about his son to his face but giving an entirely different story behind his back. He stated that he had now sent his son to school in Sydney "where I trust he will be more fortunate in his teacher" and that he fully intended to withdraw his other boys from the school. He also asked to be removed from the school committee.

Two years later he wrote to 'Mr Graham' in Brisbane asking him for a position for his son John in one of his firms, or a bank. He stated: "I am aware of the importance of a business training if he is to be anything better than a stockman."

In 1886 he applied to purchase a portion of Crown Land, about 60-70 acres, situated between his freehold land of 105 Barkers Creek and Mondue Road.

In 1890 he sold some land at Nanango and purchased two portions of Crown Land at Coolabunia. If I read this correctly, he purchased this land in order to gain convenient access to his freehold portion of '105 Booie'. In true Archibald style, his knowledge of the law enabled him to request a proportionate reduction in the deed and survey fees because the amendment act of 1889 had come into force. A month later he claimed £20/12/6 for improvements, for 60 chains of fencing.

While at Barcaldine he filled the roles of Police Magistrate, Clerk of Petty Sessions, Assistant Land Agent and Beer Duty Officer, among others.

Three years later, in 1898, he went to St. George, and filled similar roles until 1903, covering a broad district that included Barcaldine, Blackall, Aramac and Balonne.

Archibald finally moved to Brisbane as Clerk of the Home Department early in 1903 but was later that year retired at the age limit with six months leave of absence at half-pay – all part of a major reorganisation and restructure of the Home Secretary's Department. He lived there until the date of his death aged 78 in Toowong in 1916. His wife Margaret had died in Brisbane in 1902.

He was living at the home of son Francis and his wife Winifred, along with Bertram and Fred, at Bellevue Terrace St Lucia in 1903, but by 1905 he, Bertram and Fred were all living at Emma Street (possibly in Red Hill). By 1913 he was living with Fred at Glen Road in Toowong.

Archibald and Margaret had eight children, listed below.

James (John) Archibald Lee (1866–1928)

John was born at Wallumbilla Station in 1866. The family moved to Nanango in the early 1870s and John became a farmer in the district. Various records show him having lived at Ridgemere, Bylong and Broadmere. For over 25 years he was a member of the Nanango Shire Council, and for many years its chairman.

He married Florence Margaret Graham in 1896 and they had three children:

- Margaret Frances Florence b. 1897 (married George Pledger)
- Beatrice Norma b. 1902 (married Alben Perrett)
- Graham Stanley (1904-1969) (married Violet Beck in 1900).

Aged 62, John died on 27 October 1928 at the Kingaroy General Hospital. My Grandfather Frederick was the executor of his estate.

Joseph Deuchar Lee (1867 – 1937)

Joseph was born at Wallumbilla Station in 1867 and moved with his family to Nanango in the early 1870s. In 1900 he married Mary Isobel Eades at All Saints in Brisbane and they had two daughters, Hilda and Nancy. In 1905 the family was living at Brisbane Street (possibly in Brisbane) and from there they went to Victoria. Joseph was a banker, and from 1910-1932 was the manager of the Commercial Bank of Australia in Kingaroy, where he died in 1937. He had retired in 1932 and had carried on business as a commission agent. He was a foundation member of the School of Arts, was actively connected with the Citizens' Band, Kingaroy Jockey Club, and Church of England, and was a trustee of the repatriation committee.

Ethel Gertrude Lee (1870 – 1873)

Ethel, Archibald's only daughter, was born at Warwick and died of bronchitis at Nanango at the age of three.

Francis William Lee (1872 – 1944)

Francis was born at Nanango, and in 1900 married Winifred McMahon. He became an accountant with New Zealand Loan. Their only daughter was Winora Evel (Nora) who died in May 1917 aged 6 years and is buried in grave of her Grandmother Margaret Fraser Lee in the Toowong cemetery. Francis died aged 71 at Ridgemere, Nanango.

Bertram Fraser Lee (1875 – 1916)

Born at Nanango, Bertram enlisted during the first World War where he was killed in 1916 and is buried in the Warlencourt British Cemetery in France. Warlencourt British Cemetery is a Commonwealth War Graves Commission burial ground for military personnel who died on the Western Front during World War I. It is located in the Pas-de-Calais region of France. Established in 1919 to consolidate several smaller cemeteries, it was designed by Sir Edwin Lutyens and is administered by the Commonwealth War Graves Commission. There are 3,450 soldiers interred, of which 1,823 are unidentified.

Shortly before his death, Archibald (Bertram's father) received a short account of Bertie's first charge on enemy trenches. He and the Queenslanders he was with attacked the Germans and succeeded in gaining two lines, first and second, which they held for four days, when they were relieved after repulsing two counter-attacks and taking some prisoners. Bertram was killed two weeks later, after Archibald had died.

In Memory of
Private
Bertram Fraser Lee

4163, 25th Bn., Australian Infantry, A.I.F. who died on 05 November 1916 Age 41

Son of Archibald and Margaret Fraser Lee. Native of Nanango, Queensland.

Remembered with Honour
Warlencourt British Cemetery

Commemorated in perpetuity by
the Commonwealth War Graves Commission

Bertram Fraser Lee

Herbert Stanley Lee (1879 – 1944)

Herbert was born in Nanango in 1879 and married Alice Beatrice Colvin Clark in 1907. They had two children, William Stanley (1908-1993) and Martha Beatrice (1910-1964). A farmer, Herbert died at Ridgemere in Nanango in 1944.

George Arnold Lee (1879-1954)

George was born Nanango in 1879 and married Mabel Elsie Violet Colles in 1914. They had two children: Bernard Allen Lee (1916-?), and Clare Colles Lee (1919-1964). George was living at Acacia Ridge Farm when his brother Fred's family retired there in 1937. His son Bernard married Ruby Yeates, from the Yeates family mentioned by my mother during her Sandy Creek school days. By the time of his death, he was living in Walnut St, Wynnum, a coastal suburb of Brisbane.

Frederick Septimus Lee (see below)

Archibald's youngest son, Frederick Lee, was my Grandfather.

Frederick Septimus Lee (1881-1956)

My grandfather Fred was born in Nanango in 1881. He trained as an accountant and worked for most of his life with New Zealand Loan and Mercantile Agency.

In 1903 he was living with his father and two brothers at Bellevue Terrace in Brisbane, and in 1905 he and his father and brother were at Emma Street. By 1913 he (a salesman for NZ Loan by this time) and his father were living at Glen Road, Toowong; Bertram presumably had enlisted by then.

Fred's company photo

His first marriage was to Annie Margaret Grieve in 1918, but she died of influenza in 1925. By that time, he was living at 28 Sefton Avenue, Clayfield, Brisbane, next door to my grandmother's home. Annie was the daughter of Robert Grieve, who had at one time been the manager of a pastoral property known as Kurrawah in the Darling Downs and had died horribly in 1916 when he was struck by a train. His obituary read, in part:

> Mr Grieve was a quiet and unassuming in his demeanour, but was possessed of a personality that had a widespread influence for good. His sterling integrity and his frank hospitality had secured for him an extensive circle of warm and firm friends. In pastoral pursuits, Mr Grieve was recognised as a first class authority, and for many years he managed Mr Frank Brodribb's Kurrowah Station, with conspicuous ability. Condamine Plains where he had interests, also know him as a sheep and cattle expert. He was a Member of the Millmerran Shire Council, and had the respect and esteem of all classes of the community.

Robert Grieves, obituary, from our family papers

Fred was best man at Annie's sister Jean's wedding to Captain AG Stumm, so it is possible that is how he came to meet Annie.

The next electoral record from 1925 shows him living with his wife Annie at Tareen, Ascot Avenue, Clayfield. They must have moved to Sefton Avenue shortly after this, because my mother always said that my grandmother Ivy and Annie had been good friends before Annie died. Fred inherited land at Stanley, Toombul (Brisbane), from Annie when she died.

In 1928 Fred was living at the Seaview Hotel in Sandgate (Brisbane). Constructed in what was Sandgate's main street for almost 100 years, the Seaview was one of the township's leading hotels in the late 19th and early 20th centuries and continued to operate until 2014.

Fred was 49 when he married my grandmother, Alice Ivy Pointon, in 1930, and they quickly had three children and continued living at 28 Sefton Avenue in Clayfield.

Fred and Ivy, shortly after their marriage

In 1935 after the death of his friend Arthur Youngman, of Taabinga near Kingaroy, Fred held in trust the title to Youngman's property along with Arthur's wife.

Fred retired from New Zealand Loan in 1937 – according to my Mother, by this time he owned three farms in the Nanango area, so it was logical that the family should move to that area. Two farms were side by side and Mum said they were managed by Fred's brother, George and a cousin, Stan. Fred built a new house on one of the two farms, Acacia Ridge, and the family moved there.

By the end of 1937 they were well established at Acacia Ridge at Nanango, where Fred was the 'gentleman farmer' as described by my mother.

Fred at Acacia Ridge

The electoral records for 1949 show an abundance of Lees in the Nanango area.

- Acacia Ridge: Frederick Septimus and Alice Ivy Lee (my grandparents).
- Appin and Fitzroy streets, Nanango: Alice Beatrice Lee (home duties). She was Fred's brother Herbert's widow.
- Kingaroy: Mary Isabel Lee (home duties). She was Fred's brother Joseph's widow.
- Ridgemere, Nanango: Winifred Honora Lee. She was Fred's brother Frances' widow.
- Broadmere: Graham Stanley and Violet Madeleine Lee, as well as Florence Margaret Lee - Graham was Fred's nephew (brother John's son).
- Glenmore, Broadwater: William Stanley and Mary Lee. William was Fred's nephew, brother Herbert's son.
- Kingaroy, Belle Street: Edward Joseph Lee (watchmaker). Not sure who he was.

- Kingaroy: Frederick William Lee (commission agent). Not sure who he was.
- Kingaroy, Alice Street: Harold Edward Lee (mechanic). Not sure who he was.
- Kingaroy, Venman Street: George Henry Lee (labourer) and Gladys Susan Lee (peanut grader). Not sure who they were.
- Kingaroy, Belle Street: Veronica May Lee (home duties). Not sure who she was.
- Booie Rd, Nanango: Francis Allen Lee (Francis was son of Fred's brother Francis).

By 1954, there were two additional Lees on the electoral records list:

- Kingaroy, Fisher Street: Bessie Lee (home duties).
- Broadmere: John Archibald Lee (station hand).

Ivy Lee in later years

My Grandfather, Frederick Lee, died in 1956, aged 75. Ivy lived for another eighteen years. It seems that she left the farm almost straight after Fred's death, because the 1958 electoral rolls show her as living at Darnoch Tce in Highgate Hill in Brisbane, with her daughter Nancy. In the same street lived William and Ethel Lee. Fred's brother Herbert had a son William, but I do not think this is the same person.

By 1963 the electoral roll shows Ivy as living at 121 Lutwyche Rd, Windsor in Fortitude Valley – this location is now underneath a road network. In 1968 she is listed at 1 Armytage St., Lota, which is situated on the Brisbane River.

She travelled to Western Australia several times to visit her daughter Ruth on Kanandah Station, as well as spending time with both Fred and Nancy. Her final years were spent in the Jindalee Nursing Home, until she died at the age of 82.

Fred and Ivy's memorial stone

The Allan family

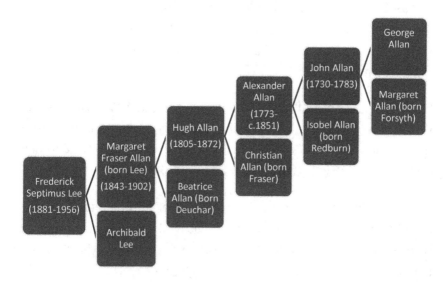

Surprisingly, despite the relatively common name with many spelling variations, I have been able to trace the Allan family back to the late 1600s in Scotland, but without substantial verification. Our connection with this family occurred with the marriage of Margaret Fraser Allan to my great grandfather, Archibald Lee. The Scottish tendency to use family names as children's second names is certainly a help when tracing family trees.

This surname is spelled interchangeably as 'Allan' or 'Allen' in historical records, but for consistency I have chosen 'Allan'.

The Scottish Allan Family

The Scottish ancestors of this family came from the area north of Aberdeen (the 'granite city' in north-east Scotland), beginning in Banffshire and gradually moving southward to Aberdeen. Banffshire, also called Banff, extends from the Grampian mountains to the North Sea. The north-eastern portion of the county, including the historic county town (seat) of Banff, is part of the council area of Aberdeenshire, while the remainder of the county lies within the council area of Moray. Despite its rugged isolation, in Banffshire there is considerable evidence of prehistoric human habitation, particularly near the coastal area. Also in the area are the ruins of several medieval castles and the 12th century kirk of Gamrie. The region remained largely Roman Catholic after the Reformation (16th century) and suffered greatly in the ensuing struggles. During the 17th century Wars of the Three Kingdoms, Banffshire was a Royalist stronghold. The industrial revolution of the 18th and 19th centuries made little impact on the mostly agricultural county.

George Allan (c. 1695-?)

George Allan, our earliest identifiable ancestor, was born in about 1695 in the parish of Marnoch, Banffshire. George married Margaret Forsyth (1685-?) on 29 Jul 1714 at Grange, Banff, and they had nine children.

Grange is a parish in the Scottish county of Moray, south west of Banff, that dates back to a royal charter granting the lands to the abbots and monks of Kinloss in 1196. Originally Grange formed a part of the parish of Keith, from which it was separated in the year 1618. Although there is no settlement apart from farms within that area, it still retains its distinct community character with its own parish church and primary school. The church was built in 1795, and it is situated within a mile of the border of the parish, on the site of the old castle once occupied by the abbots of Kinloss.

Founded in 1150 by King David I, Kinloss Abbey had 24 abbots. The abbey became one of the largest and wealthiest religious houses in Scotland. The most notable Abbot was Robert Reid, who was appointed abbot in 1528. One of his first moves as abbot was to ask the Italian scholar, Giovanni Ferrerio of Piedmont to come to Kinloss to establish a centre of academic excellence. He introduced organised education, erecting a new library and other buildings at the abbey. The remains of the abbey are now situated within a graveyard owned by the local authority.

I came across an online document entitled *Some History of the Parish of Grange,* which recounted a couple of fascinating stories from Grange. Below is an abridged version of the first story.

> *"One of the Scottish Kings (Alfred?) was boar hunting at Kinloss and was wounded. The monks of Kinloss Abbey nursed him back to health and as a reward he gave them any part of the surrounding countryside as their 'Grange Lands', which meant farm lands. They chose the valley of the Isla to the Deveron, as they judged it the most fertile valley. This is why the Parish of Grange is a long narrow strip. They built the Abbot's Castle where the Grange Church now stands, there being a handy ditch to fill the moat. They built a nunnery where the Grange churchyard now is and the nuns carried their water from the well at the side of the main road. It was supposed to be Holy water and was called the "Well of the Lady" – hence Ladywell, and above it is Ladyhill. The monks from the Castle or Abbey must have been buried in the grounds surrounding it, as a skull was discovered in recent years, after some of the old trees were blown down in a gale. This was when Sir James Innes' people were buried and it is walled in with a gate for entry.*

At the time the 'Wolf of Badenoch[5]' was raiding and burning the churches, the monks were supposed to have buried the Abbey silver under where the Grange Church now stands and there was some talk of the Lord Lion of Scotland coming with archaeological students to try and recover it but this never materialised."[6]

Lime was extensively manufactured in this parish, and most of the farms still have their own lime kilns. In 1996 the Grange community celebrated its 800 years, and a book was commissioned to document its history, however I have not been able to find this book.

Children of George and Margaret:

- George Allan (1715-?)
- Margaret Allan (1717-?)
- William Allan (1719-?)
- Isobell Allan (1721-?)
- Barbara Allan (1723-?)
- Alexander Allan (1725-?)
- Jean Allan (1727-?)
- **John Allan** (1730-1783) – our ancestor, see below
- Joseph Allan (1732-?)
- Mary Allan (1736-?).

---

[5] Alexander Stewart, Earl of Buchan, also called the Wolf of Badenoch (1343 – 1405), was the third surviving son of King Robert II of Scotland.

[6] Author unknown, *Some History of the Parish of Grange*, http://kadhg.org.uk/d/wp-content/uploads/2014/07/A_History_of_the_Parish_of_Grange_by_anon.pdf sourced December 2020

John Allan (1730-1783)

John was born in 1730 and christened on 18 April 1730 at Grange, Banff.

He married Isobel Reburn on 10 February 1756 at Grange and they appear to have had at least six children, although some of the dates of birth are a bit questionable.

- George Allan (1764-?)
- Joseph Allan (1768 -?)
- John Allan (1770-?)
- **Alexander Allan** (1773-?) our ancestor, see below
- Jannet Allan (1777-?)
- James Allan (1779-?)

War with England characterised the period of John's life, which was a period of considerable change. Pressures by the central government to change land ownership patterns in Scotland had been creating a country of mixed property ownership patterns for centuries, and common land was being privatised. The failure of the 1715 and 1745 Jacobite Risings, culminating in the Battle of Culloden, broke the power of the clans in Scotland, fostering many changes. New roads were being built to better facilitate mobility leading to transformation of settlement patterns. Planned villages were being developed. Our Allan family mostly worked on farms, probably as a mix of laborers, small tenant holders, and artisans.

This was the period of Scottish history brought to life in Diana Gabaldron's epic novels beginning with *Cross Stitch*, and later brought to the screen in the television series *Outlander*.

Alexander Allan (1773- before 1851)

Next in line, Alexander Allan was born in Scotland, presumably Grange, and married Christina Fraser (1785-1872) in Keith, Banffshire on 30 Mar 1800. She was the daughter of Hugh Fraser and Isobel Mitchell and had been born in Keith. The Fraser name recurred in subsequent generations.

In the 1841 census, Alexander is listed as a blacksmith, and he and Christina were living at Newhills, about five miles north of Aberdeen. Alexander had died by the time of the next census in 1851, as Christina is listed as resident at Skene, living with her daughter-in-law Anne and three children. In 1871 she was still in Skene, living with her son, James. Skene is a small farming community about 10km west of Aberdeen.

Alexander and Christina had the following children.

- **Isobel Donaldson (born Allan) (1801-1888):** Isobel was born at Grange, Banff In August 1801. She married Alexander Donaldson, a ferrier and carter, at Rathven in 1824 and had seven children. They were living at Rathven in 1851 and 1861, and had moved to Buckie as retirees by 1871. In 1881 Isobel was living with her son Alexander.
- **Jane Wilson/Bennett (born Allan) (1803-1890):** There are several possible marriages which might be Jane. The most interesting possibility is that she married John Wilson in 1827, and they had five children before John died in 1844. Jane then married a Mr Bennett in 1851 and emigrated to Ontario, Canada in 1855 where her husband died in 1860. In 1871, she was living at Oxford South, Ontario with her son Andrew. He died in 1874 and she lived at Woodstock, Ontario until 1890.
- **Hugh Allan (1805-1872):** Hugh Allan is our ancestor – see the next section of this chapter.
- **Alexander Allan (1806-?):** Alexander was born in Keith in August 1806. Most likely he was a wool reel master living at College Street Old Machar (now part of Old Aberdeen), and by 1841 had married Isabella (possibly Isabella Hood). They appear to have had two children, but there were many

marriage possibilities and it is difficult to narrow them down.

- **James Allan (1808-1889):** James was born in Keith, September 1808, and married Ann Humphrey in March 1838. In 1841, James, a painter, and Ann lived in Moray with children William, Robert, Anne, James and Jane. Ann is the daughter-in-law his mother Christina was living with in 1851, in Skene. He was not with Ann at the time of the 1851 census, and it is possible that he was a lodger, and agricultural labourer, at Turriff. However, James and Ann are together again in 1861 in Skene, and again in 1871 and Christina (88) is with them. By 1861 James was a landholder of five acres, with several employees. In 1881, he was most likely a pauper in the St Nicholas City Poor House. He does not appear in any further census records.

- **Elspeth Paterson (born Allan) (1818-1895):** Elspeth is believed to have married Robert Paterson, although I cannot find either a birth or a marriage record. In the 1841 census she is living with her parents at Newhills in Aberdeenshire. In 1851, she and Robert are living at Gateside, Newhills with four children (Margaret, George, Janet and Christian). In 1861 they are at Petercutler with children Janet, Christina, Mary, Jane and Elspet and two other people. In 1871 she is back at Newhills, using her maiden name of Allan, along with children Mary, Jane and Elspet. The last census in which she appears is in 1891, when she is a housekeeper, aged 73, in the house of George McAllan and Ann McRobbie. Robert had died in 1872.

Elspeth Paterson, death certificate

- **George Allan** (1824-1900): George was born in Rathven, Banff in 1824. He was living with the family at Newhills in 1841, and in 1851 he was a farm labourer at Newton of Mountblairy. In 1857 he married Isabelle Ramsay in Edinburgh. By the 1871 census they were living in Aberdeen with daughter Jean, aged 12. In 1881 he was a carter in far northern Scotland at Wick, Caithness, with Isabelle and Jean (now listed as Jane). They were all still there in 1891 and his occupation is listed in the census as 'Goods Suped Seedmer Co'. This is the last listing for George.

Hugh Allan (1805-1872)

Our ancestor Hugh is the family member who made the trip to Australia. He was born in Inchmarnock, Aberdeenshire, which I think is north west of Aberdeen – it is definitely not the island of Inchmarnock, which is off the western coast of Scotland.

On December 8, 1839, at age 29, he arrived in Australia on the Kinnear, which was the same ship the Deuchar family sailed on. I am not sure if he knew the Deuchars prior to leaving Aberdeenshire, or whether he met them on the ship, but either way his future in Australia was intertwined with this family. I think it is probable that they had both been recruited by the North British Australasian Loan and Investment Company. Hugh was listed as single, an agriculturalist from Aberdeenshire, Presbyterian, and able to read and write. The ship records show him as being 'imported by' W.C. Botts Esq, who was a shipping agent.

Hugh Allan – arrival record

Hugh and the Deuchars arrived at Sydney on a hot summer December Monday. The newspapers of the day carried an exciting description of a recent exploratory expedition which had reached the Cape at the north-east coast of Australia, as well as the capture of Robert Franks, the robber of the Yass mail. A news article enticingly described the district of New England, where the party was soon to be headed, as looking 'delightful', in the midst of a fine season with grass and water in abundance, cattle thriving and a 'never better drop of lambs'.

It is likely that Hugh first went to work at Lochinvar in NSW for three years later it is there that he married Beatrice Deuchar, whom he had probably met on the ship. His daughter Margaret, and our ancestor, was born at Lochinvar a year later.

Hugh was running a property north of Lochinvar (about a mile from Luskintyre), as there were frequent newspaper references to lost stock, various employees and his vineyard. It is probable that his property was called 'Lochinvar Estate'. He was also associated with a property called 'St Clair', which may have been near Singleton.

It is also likely that whilst at Lochinvar he became further involved with the North British Australasian Loan and Investment Company, frequently known as the 'Scotch Company' or the 'Aberdeen Company'. He was almost certainly working for the Company during the 1840s, as the number of advertisements he placed in the *Maitland Mercury* suggest a scope of responsibilities well beyond just managing a property.

Hugh spent much of the rest of his life in the employment of this company, mostly as the manager of a boiling-down plant (now known as a rendering plant) at Ipswich. He was appointed in 1848, because the following notice appeared in the *Moreton Bay Courier* in December 1848.

NOTICE.

THE undersigned having been appointed by the ABERDEEN COMPANY to Superintend a

BOILING-DOWN ESTABLISHMENT,

on a large scale, in this district, hereby gives notice that he will immediately commence the erection of the premises at a spot on the South side of the Bremer River, about 1½ or 2 miles below Ipswich. It is expected that the works will be completed in about February next. Full particulars of terms, &c., will be given in a future advertisement.

The undersigned is prepared to enter into engagements for the incoming season.

HUGH ALLAN.

Ipswich, Dec. 1, 1848.

Notice of the establishment of the boiling down works, 1848

From then he advertised frequently for stock, etc, in the local newspapers. Examples of some of these advertisements appear below. It seems that the establishment was named the 'Warrel Steaming Establishment' as this name appears as the header of some of Hugh's advertising. By December 1849 the establishment had been extended, and had a steaming capacity of 300 bullocks or 3,000 sheep per week, at the following prices:

- cattle, including curing hides, 8 shillings per head
- sheep, with tongues and feet, including packing skins, seven pence per head
- casks, 40 shillings per ton – freight paid to Brisbane; men and horses in charge of stock supplied with rations and grass.

TO STAND AT IPSWICH,
THE ENTIRE HORSE *B Y R O N*, got
by Gratis, out of a three-quarter bred Mare.
Terms—£2, groomage included.
HUGH ALLAN.
Ipswich, 28th Nov., 1848.

£1 REWARD.
LOST, from the Long Pocket, about a month
back, a Bay MARE, switch tail, star on the
forehead, branded   N
HA.
The above reward will be paid on her delivery
to Mr. Hugh Allan, Ipswich.
22nd January, 1849.

WANTED IMMEDIATELY,
A COOPER who thoroughly understands the
business. A single man will be preferred.
Apply at Warell Boiling-down Establishment,
near Ipswich.
HUGH ALLAN.
20th December, 1849.

Examples of some of Hugh Allan's advertisements

In February 1850, a dreadful accident occurred at the plant when an eight-year-old girl, the daughter of one of the plant's employees, was putting a stick in the fire and her clothing caught alight. She died a day later.

Theft was also a problem for the establishment as, in May 1850, Hugh offered a £10 reward for the conviction of thieves who were stealing hobbles off the horses at the establishment.

By 1862, Hugh Allan had an association with St Ruth's Station, and was listed as 'Superintendent'. St Ruth is a locality split between the Western Downs and the Toowoomba region. St Ruth's was taken up as part of Cecil Plains pastoral run by Henry Stuart Russell in 1842. It was separated from Cecil Plains in 1842 by Richard Jones, probably for the Aberdeen Company, which explains Hugh Allan's later association. There must have been some financial trouble in 1862, because an advertisement in the *Toowoomba Chronicle* in March of that year called for parties having any account against the station to send the details to Hugh Allan. The troubles evidently continued, because a year later there was a notice that all parties found on the run collecting stock without permission would be prosecuted. It is probable that he was living at St Ruth's station, because his daughter Margaret married Archibald Lee there in 1863.

Hugh Allan[7]

---

[7] This image appears in Fox, Matthew J (1923). *The history of Queensland : its people and industries : an historical and commercial review descriptive and*

By August 1867, he had an association with Wallumbilla as there is an insolvency notice for Hugh Allan. This is interesting, because George Deuchar and Archibald Lee at Wallumbilla Station were in financial trouble by this time and desperately trying to clear the station's debts – eventually being foreclosed in May 1868. Hugh's wife Beatrice was George's niece, plus they all had an association with the Aberdeen Company, so there must be a connection with Hugh's insolvency.

In December 1867, the *Toowoomba Chronicle* reported that the report of the official assignee showed that Hugh's debts amounted to £689/10/10.

A few months later, in February 1868, Hugh's youngest daughter Mary, married Robert Douglas Jnr., from the Kilmorey Station, one of the stations owned by Deuchar and Lee, and at this time the full-time residence of George Deuchar. The couple were married by Archbishop Glennie at Glengallan.

Two months after that, his second daughter, Beatrice Deuchar Allan married William Forbes Gordon from Manar, NSW – they were also married at the Deuchar property at Glengallan.

It seems that despite his apparent insolvency, Hugh continued as the manager of the Warrell Boiling Down Works because in 1872, when William Leslie and his friend Peter Murray were taking an Arab horse he had bought in India to his brother George Leslie, they spent a couple of days with "Hugh Allen, at the Aberdeen Company's Boiling Down Works." It was reported that all three men were Aberdonians and school mates.[8]

---

biographical facts, figures and illustrations: an epitome of progress. Brisbane: States Publishing Company, page 219

[8] 1872 – Extract from *The Early History of Warwick District and Pioneers of the Darling Downs*

A year later, in January 1873, Hugh was tragically killed when he fell from a dray. The wheel had passed over his thigh, breaking the bone and severing an artery. The following obituary appeared in the Maryborough Chronicle:

> DISTRESSING FATAL ACCIDENT.—The *War-wick Examiner* of Saturday says:—" No doubt many of our readers will be very sorry to hear of the sudden death, under very distressing circumstances, of Mr. Hugh Allan, for many years in charge of stations in this colony and New South Wales for the North British Australasian Company. The deceased gentleman was proceeding with his teams from Womblebank; when about six miles from Tooloombilla, and while driving one of them, he fell, the horses and dray passing over him, and breaking his thigh. The man with him at once started for assistance, and very soon came back with Mr. George Deuchar (a connexion of the deceased) and a buggy, but too late to be of any assistance, as the unfortunate gentleman had expired meanwhile from loss of blood, an artery having been severed. Dr. Fullerton, J.P., held an enquiry, and he was buried at Tooloombilla. Mr. Allan was a very old colonist, and much respected by all who knew him."

Hugh Allan, obituary

Children of Hugh and Margaret Allan

- **Margaret Fraser Allan** (1843-1902): was born in Lochinvar, is our ancestor and she married Archibald Lee at St Ruth's station in May 1863 – see below
- **Beatrice Deuchar Allan** (1846-1917): In 1868 she married **William Forbes Gordon** who was born 19 September 1843 in Goulburn, NSW to Hugh Gordon (1816-1857) and Mary King Macarthur (1822-1898). He died in August 1904 in 'Manar', Braidwood, NSW of Bright's disease. He had taken

over the Manar estate when his father died. He and Beatrice had ten children, three of whom predeceased him.

Beatrice died aged 71 and was buried in the family burial ground at Manar.

Manar, near Braidwood, NSW[vii]

Manar, near Braidwood, NSW is an estate of nearly 11,000 acres acquired by William's father, Hugh Gordon, in 1841, and named after Manar in Aberdeenshire, Scotland. The Leslies of Warthill House, Aberdeenshire, Scotland, were friends and neighbours of the Gordons of Manar and members of both families had migrated to Australia during the 1830s. Hugh Gordon was very ill both before and during the voyage and on arriving was cared for by the Hannibal MacArthur family at Paramatta. Two of the Leslies married daughters of Hannibal, and Hugh married Mary, another of Hannibal's daughters. He bought the property 'Redesdale', near Braidwood in 1841 and renamed it 'Manar'. Hugh built the house adjacent to a previous cottage, and had the staircase constructed to resemble the staircase in his childhood home in Aberdeenshire.

- **Mary Ann Deuchar Allan** (1849-1941): Mary Ann married Robert Douglas from Kilmorey Station in February 1868. The Douglas family originated in the highlands of Scotland, and this Robert was best known for his time on Mt Maria Station near Morven.

His father (also Robert) had long been involved in pastoral interests, having run away from home and shipped on board a whaler at the age of 10, and then spending several years as part of the mercantile marine before finally coming to Australia at the age of 21. Even his trip to Australia was eventful, when it became evident that the drunkard captain was incapable of navigating the vessel and Robert Douglas volunteered to take over as commander. Once in Australia he became a jackaroo in the Hunter district before taking over Redback Station. He sold out in 1855 and established a soap factory at Kangaroo Point.

His son, Robert, the eventual husband of Mary Ann Allan, had followed a bush life in the Dawson and Maranoa districts before becoming manager of Wallumbilla Station for Archibald Lee, his brother-in-law. In 1875 he settled at Mt Maria – for the first four months the family lived in a 'gunya', an Aboriginal home made of wood and bark – which eventually became a very successful cattle station. They had three sons and seven daughters.

Mary McManus made the following observation about the Douglas family:

"Mr. Robert Douglas is one of the old pioneer squatters, and during the early days he and Mrs.

Douglas had their full share of all the hard work and roughing of a squatter and housekeeper on stations at that time, and anyone who had experienced them as they did will know they were not by any means light or easy, especially when rearing a young family. This rough life was especially severe on one who had been brought up so quietly as Mrs. Douglas was, and so unused as she was in her early girlhood to anything of that kind of life, but she battled with all these difficulties bravely, her life in the bush at that time being a sample of that led by many a squatter's and working man's wife and daughter, and they, like Mrs. Douglas overcame them all successfully."[9]

Margaret Fraser Allan 1843-1902

Margaret Fraser Allan had been born at Lochinvar in NSW but grew up at Warrell, near Ipswich, when her father moved there to run the boiling down works in 1848. Her mother was a member of the Deuchar family, so it can be assumed that through their association with the Deuchars, she met Archibald Lee who had spent time working at Glengallan.

Archibald Lee and George Deuchar had already begun establishing Wallumbilla Station when he married Margaret at St Ruth's Station in 1863, so the newly married Margaret would have found herself in a remote, greenfields area, establishing a new station settlement – just as her granddaughter Ruth Lee did so many years later.

---

[9] Mary A McManus (1902) *Reminiscences of the Early Settlement of the Maranoa District.*

How challenging life must have been for the newly married Margaret. Stores, for example, had to be ordered months ahead and last for many more months. I was fascinated by the following order for Wallumbilla in October 1863, as recorded in Archibald Lee's letter book:

- 100 lbs hops
- 20 lbs pepper
- 2 boxes raisins
- 1 ton ration sugar in casks
- 1 ton salt in sound casks
- 1 chest tea
- 2-3 tons ration flour
- 1 piece of bed ticking
- 1 piece of towelling
- 3 doz Crimean shirts
- 1 doz assorted thread, brown and black
- 20 lbs washing soda
- 5 lbs blue
- 2 doz white felt hats
- 1 doz one ring hobble chains
- 6 oz strychnine
- 3 gross wax matches – large sized boxes
- 2 gross Holloways pills
- 1 doz pairs Wellington boots (good)
- 2 tins sago
- 1 case pipes (good).

Her first two sons, James and Joseph were born at Wallumbilla. It must have been with some relief that the family moved to Warwick and then on to Nanango after the troubled final years of their time at Wallumbilla Station, and they stayed there for the next 23 years.

Her only daughter Ethel, who died at the age of three, was born in Warwick, and sons Francis, Bertram, Herbert, George and my grandfather Frederick, were all born at Nanango.

I can't help wondering if Margaret and Archibald lived separately in their later years, as there are few references to them as being together. However, I did find the following reference to them both in *Queensland Figaro* in October 1901: "Mr A. Lee, police magistrate, St George, accompanied by Mrs Lee, arrived in town on Tuesday." Archibald was based at St George when Margaret died, aged 59, of pneumonia in July 1902, but she was living at Langshaw Street, New Farm in Brisbane.

The following obituary appeared in *The Brisbane Courier* on 3 July 1902:

The many friends of Mr. A. Lee, Police Magistrate, St. George, formerly of Nanango, will be grieved to hear of the sad death of his wife early yesterday morning, after only a very short illness. Mrs. Lee leaves seven sons, three of whom are married—John and Stanley, of Ridgemere, Nanango ; Joseph, of the Commercial Bank of Australia, Melbourne ; Frank and Frederick, of the New Zealand Loan and Mercantile Agency Company, Brisbane ; Bertram, of Dalgety and Co., Brisbane ; and George, who has only recently been transferred to the Queensland National Bank, Townsville. Mrs. Walter Scott, of Teneriffe, one of Mrs. Lee's oldest friends, was with her till the end. Dr. Jackson was in attendance throughout the deceased lady's illness. Mr. Lee, who was telegraphed for to St. George, will reach Brisbane by the mail train on Friday.

Margaret Fraser Lee, obituary

Her death certificate was certified by her son, Francis. She is buried at Toowoomba. Interestingly she seems to have died intestate – rather surprising considering her husband was a police magistrate and evidently very well versed in the law! There is a notice to creditors in the *Government Gazette* in 1903. She is shown as being the "owner of allotment 3 of suburban section 74, town of Nanango."

My mother never met her grandparents, as both passed away long before she was born, and so the details of their lives are deduced from written records. Margaret Fraser Lee's story is largely untold, overshadowed by the dominating character and presence of her husband, Archibald. After learning about the events and challenges she faced over her life, I am left with the image of a strong, quiet and supportive woman who faced many tragedies and who dedicated her life to her husband and sons.

The Deuchar Family

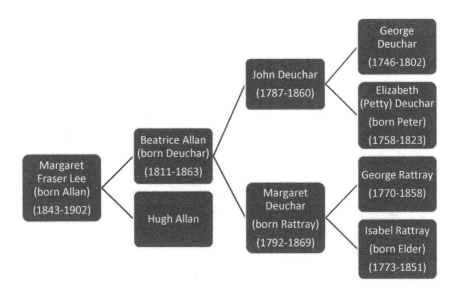

The Deuchar name is of territorial origin from the lands of Deuchar in the lordship of Fern or Fearn in Angus, Scotland. The Deuchars were considered one of the oldest families in the district and were said to have come into possession of the comparatively small area (about 200 acres) of the lands of Deuchar about the year 1230. The family are believed to have been vassals to the Lindsay family in the fourteenth century, and to have paid an annual fee of a pair of white gloves. 'Deuchar' has been used as a surname since the medieval period but is still relatively rare.

There is a fascinating story of one of the Deuchars killed in the 11th century when fighting the Danes at the Battle of Barry. His body was able to be identified because of the longer coffin, and because he was of 'gigantic stature' and had six fingers and toes on each hand and foot. There is also a story of a family sword, famously reputed to having been used to cut off a boar's head, and then centuries later to have been shortened to accommodate a user of diminutive stature.[10]

The Deuchars seem to have been world travellers, with several members of the family migrating to the Caribbean, and others to South Africa, Australia and New Zealand. One Alexander Deuchar, from Aberdeenshire, was a rector of St. Thomas in Barbados during the early eighteenth century.

Two family members of note were Alexander Deuchar and his brother, David, both of whom had strong associations with the Knights Templar in Scotland.

The Templar Order was first established in Scotland in 1128 and with the support of succeeding Scottish kings the Order came to possess considerable property. In Scotland, the Order has never been banned or abolished, but remained under the protection of the king of Scotland. The Order had been publicly operating as The Order of St John and the Temple (Scotland 1314) and this branch of the Order was considered defunct when the Preceptor of the Order, Sir James Sandilands, converted to Protestantism. However, the Order didn't dissolve, it only drew back from public view and operation remained hidden for more than a hundred years mainly because it became purely Templar again. This secret functioning had not been compromised until 1689 when John Graham of Claverhouse known as 'Bonnie Dundee' was killed in the battle of Killiecrankie.

In 1737, Templar Knight Andrew Michael Ramsay, and Scot from Ayr and Prince Charles Edward Stuart's tutor, gave a public speech

---

[10] David McGregor Peter (1856) *The Baronage of Angus and Mearns, Oliver and Boyd*, Tweedale Court, Edinburgh, p67 (Note: this book was withdrawn from circulation soon after it was issued, but has been digitized, and is available at https://electricscotland.com/history/forfar/baronageofangus.pdf)

in Paris. In his speech, he claimed that Freemasonry had spread among the Crusaders and that they had founded the Lodge of St John. Charles Edward Stuart known also as 'Bonnie Prince Charlie' was elected a new Grand Master of Scottish Knights Templar in Edinburgh in 1745. John Olivant from Bachilton became the next Grand master in 1795, followed by Alexander Deuchar.[11]

Alexander Deuchar (1777-1844) was a seal engraver and Lyon Herald at the Court of the Lord Lyon. The Deuchar family had been Jacobite but transferred their allegiance to the Hanoverian cause before 1745, when a prominent Jacobite, Lyon of Easter Ogil carried off the great sword of Deuchar (as mentioned above). The sword was recovered after the Battle of Culloden in 1746 and was in the possession of Alexander when he started his revival of the Scottish Knights Templar. The new Order started formally in 1805 when a charter was issued to Alexander. It became the Grand Assembly of Knights Templar in Edinburgh and Alexander was Grand Master.

David Deuchar was a goldsmith, seal engraver and an amateur etcher. David served in the Peninsular War (1808-14) and during the campaign in Portugal took the altar cross from the Templar Church at the Castle of Tomar which had been destroyed by the French, and presented the Cross at the inauguration of the Scottish Knights Templar Conclave. Somewhat controversially he opened the Conclave to non-Masons and issued charters to Encampments which were non-Masonic. David Deuchar was also one of the first to have spotted the talent of the future portrait painter, Henry Raeburn, encouraging him to become a painter rather than a jeweller. One of Rabeburn's portraits was of Alexander Allan.

---

[11] *The Order of the Temple in Scotland*
https://www.theknightstemplar.org/scottish-templars/ sourced November 2020.

George Deuchar (1747-1802)

The earliest Deuchar ancestor to whom I can find a direct connection was George Deuchar, who lived on the family estate at Fern, Angus, Scotland in the second half of the eighteenth century. He married Elizabeth (Petty) Peter (1758-1823) from Aberlemno in Angus, Scotland, and they had 11 children, including our ancestor John.

- William Deuchar (1769-1822)
- Elizabeth (Betty) Deuchar (1778-?)
- Margaret Deuchar (1780-?)
- George Deuchar (1781-1853) (moved to Australia, and then New Zealand)
- Son Deuchar (1783-?)
- Isabel (Bell) Deuchar (1783-?)
- Peter Deuchar (1785-1804)
- **John Deuchar** (1787-1859) (our ancestor)
- Mary Deuchar (1791-?)
- Ann Deuchar (1795-?)
- James Jefferson Deuchar (1799-1823).

George and Petty are interred in the family burial place at the old church of Fern (the vault was within the church until 1805 when the church was rebuilt) and their youngest son, James erected a monument in 1826.

The connection of the Deuchars with their lands ceased in 1819 when George's second son, *George Deuchar*, became insolvent and the lands were sold. It is not known why the lands were inherited by George, and not the first son, William. After the sale, son George for some time held the farm of Pittrichie in Aberdeenshire and, about 1830, he appears to have been inspector of cleansing (interesting job role) in Dundee and soon thereafter was land-steward at Errol Park in the carse (ward) of

Gowrie. Subsequently, he emigrated to Australia with his wife and daughters. He came out on the John Barry in 1837: George (46), wife Ann (39), and daughters Jane (19) and Ann (14). Two older sons, George Deuchar and James Jefferson Deuchar, are reputed to have remained in Scotland, and died at relatively young ages.

George snr was posted on the *John Barry* passenger list as a farmer, Presbyterian, and could read and write. Ann (his wife) died of typhus on the voyage; he had a fever and the daughters were marked as 'convalescent'. Three adults and 22 children died on this voyage and, on arrival, the ship was quarantined at North Head, Sydney.

George Deuchar left this description of the quarantine conditions:

> *"...we were landed at Spring Cove about six miles from Sydney and put under quarantine and remained there for eleven weeks. By the time we landed the fever was spreading very rapidly. We were landed and put in tents on the shore. Four weeks after our arrival I was seized with the fever and at one time the Doctors had given up all hopes of my recovery. My coffin was made and two masons began to work a head stone for me but it has pleased God to restore me to perfect good health. By the time I was able to crawl to my tent door, Jean and Ann [his daughters] was seized with fever in one day. Jean did not suffer so much as Ann. Ann's case for some time was very doubtful nor has she altogether recovered from the effects of it at present."*[12]

---

[12] The John Barry in quarantine, http://manlylocalstudies.blogspot.com/2014/08/the-john-barry-in-quarantine.html sourced December 2020

After spending some time at Singleton in the Hunter Valley, George moved to New Zealand in 1841 and died in Auckland in 1853. George was listed on an 1852 jury list as a farmer and on the electoral roll from 1853 as living at Freemans Bay. His daughter Ann also moved to New Zealand, married a tanner named McVay and died in 1892.

George's brother, *John Deuchar*, who is our ancestor, settled in Aberdeenshire, and his eldest son, John, with other members of the family, came to Australia.

John Deuchar (1787-1860?)

John was born at Deam in Kincardineshire, Scotland, midway between Edinburgh and Stirling. He married Margaret Rattray (1792-1869) on 11 Nov 1810 at Tullynessle and Forbes and Kearn, Aberdeen, Scotland. Forbes, which was formerly united with the parish of Kearn, was annexed to Tullynessle in 1811. In the 1851 census he was listed as a 'road surveyor and farmer'. Most of the family trees I accessed placed his death as 1885, but he was definitely gone by 1861, because his wife Margaret is listed on the 1861 census as a widow, living at Rubislaw Seafield, an outer suburb of Aberdeen.

They had ten children, three of whom came to Australia.

Children of John and Margaret Deuchar

- **Beatrice Deuchar** (1811-1863): Beatrice came to Australia with her brother John on the *Kinnear* in 1839. She married Hugh Allan and is our ancestor – see below.
- **Janet Deuchar** (1813-1844): Baptised in Tullynessle and Forbes and Kearn, Aberdeen, Scotland, Janet is believed to have died at the age of 21. She does not appear in the 1841 census, and I can find no record of her death.
- **Margaret Deuchar** (1815-1830): died at the age of 15

- **James Deuchar** (1817-1837?): I cannot verify the death date of 1837, aged 20, and am unable to locate anything other than his Christening records.
- **Jessie Deuchar** (1821-?): last identified as living with her parents in Kirktown 1841, aged 20
- **John Deuchar** (1820-1872): John came to Australia in 1839 on the *Kinnear* as a farm servant with his sister Beatrice, and eventually married Eliza Lee, daughter of Joseph Lee – see below.
- **George Deuchar** (1824-1890): George also came to Australia and married Louisa Jackson 1865 at Glengallan. In the 1851 census his 'son', George Jackson, was listed as living with him. However, son George was 14 at the time, which would have made his father George 12 when he was conceived, which does seem unlikely, so this relationship remains unexplained, and the 'son' does not appear to have been any relation to George's later wife, Louisa, even though they have the same surname. 'Son' George remained in Inverurie, Scotland, became a successful grocer, married Ida and had at least ten children.

Louisa Jackson had come to Australia on the ship *Duncan Dunbar* in 1861 and stayed with Robert Douglas, who later married Hugh Allan's daughter Mary Ann. Her marriage notice reports that she was the daughter of the late Edward Jackson, from Leeds. Both she and her brother James Watkin Jackson, along with four other siblings, appear in the 1841 census with their parents Edward and Jane Jackson, living in Leeds. James Jackson also came to Australia and was manager of the Australian Joint Stock Bank in Warwick. Louisa's trip to Warwick included stops at several of the established stations and she married George Deuchar in 1865 before settling at Kilmorey Station.

This was the George Deuchar who went into partnership with Archibald Lee at Wallumbilla and Kilmorey Stations. Kilmorey Run was taken up in May, 1861, by George Deuchar and Archibald Lee, who at that time owned Wallumbilla. In 1864 George Deuchar went to reside permanently at Kilmorey, where he lived for several years.

After a series of setbacks George Deuchar entered the Government service as a member of the Crown Prosecution Service and Land Commissioner at Stanthorpe, and was court/law officer from 1870 to 1890 (although on the 1874 city directory he is still listed as a grazier at Kilmorey). He died of influenza in 1890 aged 64. He and Louisa are both buried at Stanthorpe. They do not appear to have had any children.

- **Susan Deuchar** (1826-1867): Born in Bellie, Moray, Susan was living with brother George in 'Aberdeen West' in 1841 census, along with her sister Mary Ann Deuchar (22) and George's 'son', George Jackson (14). She married hay merchant Alexander Jamieson at Old Machar, Aberdeen in 1853. However, by 1861 she was presumably a widow and living with her mother Margaret (70), her sister Mary Ann's daughter Margaret (6) and two domestic servants. If the death date of 1867 is correct, she was just 43 when she died.

- **Mary Ann Deuchar** (1828-1919): Mary Ann was born at Bellie, in Moray and in 1851 (aged 22) was a housekeeper for her brother George Deuchar in Aberdeen. She married William Hunter, a coal miner, in 1853 in Aberdeen. By 1861 they were living at Inveresk with five children, and a sixth was living with her mother. A further two children had been added by 1871.

- **Margaret Deuchar** (1832-?): It was not unusual at the time to name a second child after a deceased first child, and

Margaret was named after her sister who had died two years beforehand. The second Margaret was born in Bellie, Moray and is listed as living with her father at Kirktown in 1841. The most likely marriage was to an engine driver, James Black, but the evidence is not sufficient for any certainty.

- **William Deuchar** (1835-?): born in Bellie, Moray and in 1841 was with his parents in Kirktown, Abderdeenshire, aged 6. The most likely entry for the 1851 census is as an agricultural labourer working for David Alexander in Mgcholes Bothie, Angus, but this is not a good match and it is possible that he died during childhood.

Beatrice Deuchar (1811-1863)

Born in 1811 at Tullynessle, Aberdeen, Scotland, Beatrice came to Australia on the *Kinnear* in 1839 with her brother John, aged 28, listed as a house servant who could read and write, and of Presbyterian faith. On arrival, she went to Lochinvar with her brother and it was there that she married Hugh Allan who had come out on the same ship. Their story continues in the chapter on the Allan family. Beatrice died at St Ruth Station, Dalby, and is buried at Warwick. They had three daughters.

John Deuchar (1820-1872)

John Deuchar (1822-1872)[13], was born at Aberdeen, Scotland, son of John Deuchar, farmer, and his wife Margaret, née Rattray. After migrating to New South Wales in 1839, he gained pastoral experience in the Hunter River district, and about 1842 drove

---

[13] Much of this information is taken from an article about John Deuchar which was published in Australian Dictionary of Biography, Volume 4, (MUP), 1972.

sheep from Maitland to the Darling Downs for the Aberdeen Co., later the North British Australasian Co.

From 1844 he was cattle overseer for Patrick Leslie (this is one of the Leslie brothers who had lived next door to the Gordons in Aberdeenshire – see the Allan story) at Goomburra. Patrick Leslie later bought Goomburra. Part of his published obituary included the following:

> "We have heard Mr. Hodgson on two occasions at the dinners of the Royal Agricultural Society of Queensland, tell of a characteristic incident which occurred when he first met Mr. Deuchar on the Downs, and which proves that although some of our large squatters now enjoy every luxury, their colonial experience has not always been a bed of roses, but before reaping the profits of their enterprise they had many discomforts and privations to undergo. Mr. Hodgson after a long overland journey through the wild bush came upon Mr. Deuchar's camp shortly after it was pitched, and found Mr. Deuchar frying a steak and boiling his own "billy" of tea over a log fire, and only just after the act of washing his own shirt at the river. Mr. Hodgson asked Mr. Leslie if there was any good country up the river, and the latter being desirous of securing it himself told him that there was plenty of magnificent plains down the river, which afterwards turned out to be correct, as Yandilla, Cecil Plains, &c., proved."[14]

---

[14] *Warwick Examiner*, September 14.

After two years, with support from Walter Grey of Ipswich, he bought Canal Creek, already well stocked with merinos. In 1848 Deuchar sold Canal Creek, and succeeded Fred Bracker as manager of Rosenthal for the Aberdeen Co.; he also became travelling superintendent of the company's properties. On Rosenthal, Deuchar had the first two thoroughbred merino rams on the Darling Downs: Camden Billy, already there when he took over the property, and German Billy, which he brought with him from Canal Creek. An impressive merino stud was developed from a blend of Negrette and Rambouilet strains.

Thomas Hall, early settler and recorder of the history of the Darling Downs, wrote of John Deuchar:

> *"John Deuchar was an energetic man, who spared himself very little in the supervision of this grand property, and as a consequence, was known as a man of iron constitution. Deuchar's favourite hack then was a grey mare, who, whenever she had the opportunity, would clear away from Rosenthal, and make straight for a creek near the present day South Toolburra head station."*[15]

Deuchar also began breeding cattle, especially Shorthorns, and brought to Rosenthal Lord Raglan, the first imported Shorthorn bull to reach the Downs, and well-bred cattle from the Australian Agricultural Company's properties farther south. A lover of good horseflesh and especially dependent on it for his inspections, he also developed a racing stud. His stallion, Grey Arab, bought from one of the Aberdeen Co.'s properties, sired many fine horses, some of which Deuchar rode successfully at race meetings both

---

[15] Thomas Hall (1925) *The early history of Warwick District and Pioneers of the Darling Downs*, Hall, Thomas Toowoomba. Robertson & Proven Ltd, p 35

on the flat and over the fences. He also introduced Omar Pasha, one of the first Clydesdale stallions on the Downs.

In 1855 he went into partnership with Charles H Marshall on Glengallan, also near Warwick, where he continued his work in stock breeding. His overseer, William Anderson, had been at school with him and had come to the colony on the same ship. Deuchar insisted on building up his own teams of employees; on taking over both Rosenthal and Glengallan he had dispersed the families on the properties and replaced them with other employees already known to him. Most of those displaced moved to Warwick and many became well-known pioneers of that town.

On 4 May 1857 at Paddington, Sydney, John Deuchar married Eliza Charlotte Lee, sixteen-year-old sister of Archibald Lee, and daughter of the deceased Joseph Lee.

In 1858-60 with his wife and infant daughter he visited Scotland. On his return, bringing with him eighteen German rams, he continued his developmental work at Glengallan and in 1867 built at a cost of £12,000 the impressive two-storied homestead with white stone quarried on the property.

By the mid-1860s Glengallan was well known in both Queensland and New South Wales for its high-quality stock, wool and produce. In 1867, the *Warwick Examiner* reported:

> *"One of the pleasantest places that the traveller meets coming over the Downs on his journey to Warwick is that of Glengallan, the station of John Deuchar Esq. On a slightly elevated piece of ground on the banks of a creek, commanding a view to the south-east and west of the rich undulating plains of this part of the Downs, is situated the head-station. The worthy proprietor is well known as one of the pioneers and oldest inhabitants of the Downs and through his enterprise in*

*importing at a heavy expense the best breeds of sheep
and cattle from Europe he has succeeded in producing
a description of wool which for its length and fineness
is well known amongst wool buyers at home. In
addition to the many extensive improvements which
have of late years been carried on, there is now in
course of erection a large stone mansion, which for the
style of architecture, and the substantial character if
the building, as well as ornamentation of its details,
will be one of the most splendid gentleman's
residences in the colony..."*

Warwick Examiner, Sat 9 Nov, 1867

Glengallin was first offered for sale in June 1869, a property of
36,000 acres, fully fenced, with 40,000 sheep and 500 head of
pure-bred cattle. The house alone was valued at £10,000. The
public auction was handled by Brewster and Trebeck but was
unsuccessful due to the 'excessive reserve'. John Deuchar was in
financial trouble, however, and a month later the Bank of
Australia was successful in an action to recover £5,834 from an
overdrawn bank account. The property was listed again in
December of that year, this time for sale by order of the
mortgagee, but again failed to sell. John Deuchar was announced
as insolvent the following February and at the Supreme Court
hearing in April his debts were assessed as £17,090.

The partnership with Charles Marshall had been dissolved in 1870
and Marshall was now a listed creditor. He returned to the Darling
Downs and took up residence at Glengallan which he ran until his
death during a visit to England in 1874.

The period of 1870 was a difficult time for the Deuchars. In
addition to their financial woes, extensive local flooding had

delayed the commencement of shearing, Eliza was heavily pregnant and gave birth to a daughter in June, and then in November her brother Dr Washington Lee died suddenly.

By March of 1871, John Deuchar had retired to Mile End in Warwick, where he advertised his willingness to class sheep at the rate of £2 10/- per thousand. Mile End is one of Warwick's original homesteads built in 1862. This historic brick home is surrounded by deep verandahs with sweeping views across the Condamine, over the Warwick racecourse and the town.

He died, almost penniless, of pneumonia, aged 50, on 11 September 1872, survived by his wife, two daughters and six sons. His obituary in the *Warwick Examiner* continued:

> *"Mr. Deuchar was a liberal subscriber to every charitable institution in the district, and his liberality to all, rich or poor, who called at the station, was well-known. He was a kind parent, and a good husband, and his many excellent qualities gained him the good feeling of every one with whom he came in contact. His funeral took place yesterday morning, and was very numerously attended. The corpse was removed from Mile End to St. Mark's Church, where the service was conducted by the Rev. James Love. Most of the places of business were closed during the early part of the day, and a large number of the townspeople, as well as many others from a distance, followed all that was mortal of John Deuchar to its last resting place, in the Warwick Cemetery."*

The following marble tablet was erected by friends of John Deuchar and can be found at St Mark's Anglican Church in Grafton, NSW.

Memorial tablet to John Deuchar

Children of John and Eliza Deuchar

- **Mary Anne Rattray Deuchar** (1858 -1924): married Donald Gunn (1856-1943) at St George NSW in 1880; had five children and died at Brisbane. They lived at Stanthorpe and Texas, Qld.

- **John Leafield Deuchar** (1859-1899): John was born in Scotland during the visit made by John and Eliza from 1858-60. He married Annie Marie Dawson at Canterbury NSW in 1884.

- **George Archibald Deuchar** (1861-1890): He married Alice Wolsterholme in 1920 and they had three sons.

- **William Glen Deuchar** (1864-1931): he was founder and a director of WG Deuchar and Co Ltd, shipping agents, and a prominent grazier from Bango Station, Coolalie, Yass. He married Martha Dyson in 1889 at Petersham NSW and they had one son.

- **Lindsay Deuchar** (1866-1915): He married Jane Dawson in Sydney in 1889, and they had two children, both born in Sydney. From 1900 he was the Brisbane manager of the Commercial Bank of Australia Ltd, and before then he held the position of manager of the Brunswick (Victoria) branch and had also managed several of the country and suburban offices of the bank mainly in Victoria. He was a prominent member of the Brisbane Club and was also a member of the Toowong and New Farm Bowling Clubs and had proved himself an expert at the game of bowls. His son had died while fighting with the Australian Expeditionary Force at the Dardanelles.

- **Allan Deuchar** (1867-1947): An estate agent/auctioneer, he married Ruth Annie Cowley in 1889, they had six children and he died in Heidleberg, Victoria.

- **Florence Ada Deuchar** (1870-1905): married George Waugh, of Brisbane. She possibly died from birth complications, two weeks after her son John Deuchar Neil Waugh was born in July 1905.

- **Frank Leslie Deuchar** (1872-1872): died in infancy.

The Pointon family

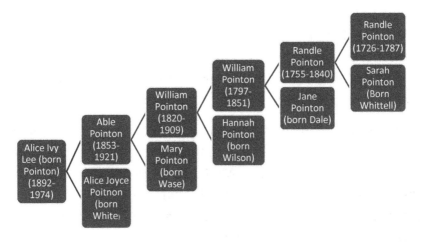

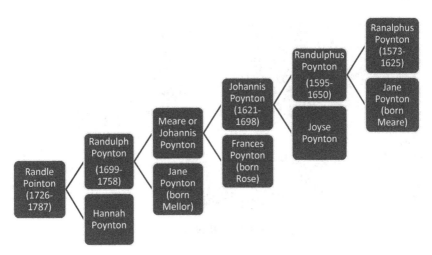

The Pointon family originates in Norton le Moors from the county of Staffordshire. The parish of Norton le Moors is located in the north-east of the city of Stoke-on-Trent, only a few miles from Wolstanton and the major city of Newcastle-under-Lyme.

Norton in the Moors, to give the village its real name, was a manor in the Hundred of Pirehill in Staffordshire and is now a mixture of urban and rural areas consisting mainly of pasture. Judging by its entry in the *Domesday Book* it could have been considerably larger than it is at present. Norton le Moors appears in the *Domesday Book* of 1086 as 'Nortone', meaning 'North town'. At the time of the *Domesday* survey, the village was held by Robert de Stafford. During the Middle Ages, the area developed due to its location on the road from Leek to Burslem, later became the Leek to Newcastle road.

Norton-in-the-Moors is where the city meets the moors, and is home to Norton Colliery. The community also played an important role in the rise of Primitive Methodism, founded by Stoke-on-Trent-born Christian converts Hugh Bourne and William Clowes, the 'ranters', hosting the third of their infamous 'camp meetings' in Norton-in-the-Moors in 1807.

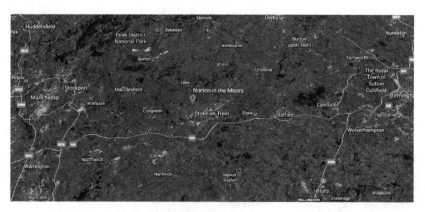

Google maps location of Norton in the Moors

St Bartholomew's Church at Norton in the Moors was founded before the end of the 12th century and was rebuilt in 1737 and, again significantly rebuilt, in 1915. To this day it remains as one of the oldest surviving buildings in the Staffordshire Potteries. Many of the Bartholomew parish records are intact and it is because of these that it is possible to trace so much information about Pointon ancestors back to the 1500s.

St Bartholomews Church, Norton in the Moors[viii]

Newcastle-under-Lyme

The major town in the region is Newcastle-under-Lyme which takes its name from the new castle erected about 1145 by Ranulf de Gernons, fourth earl of Chester, near the Lyme Forest. The castle became obsolete in Tudor times.

By the mid-18th Century our Pointon ancestors were on the move, some living in a small village (Audley) just outside Newcastle-under-Lyme, and then later living in the town itself. Others moved to Wolstanton. By this time, our Pointons were mostly master paviours, also called 'flaggers', which involved laying paving stones, etc. Most of the wider family were either potters or colliers.

Newcastle-under-Lyme is not mentioned in the 1086 Domesday Book, as it grew up around the 12th-century castle, but it must have rapidly become a place of importance because a charter was given to the town by Henry II in 1173. The new castle was built to

127

supersede an older fortress at Chesterton, about two miles to the north, although nothing remains of that.

In 1235 Henry III constituted it a free borough, granting a guild merchant and other privileges. In 1251 he leased it under a fee farm grant to the burgesses. In 1265, Newcastle-under-Lyme was granted by the Crown to Simon de Montfort, and subsequently to Edmund Crouchback, through whom it passed to Henry IV.

Newcastle-under-Lyme did not feature much in the English Civil War, except for being plundered by the Royalists. However, it was the hometown of Major-General Thomas Harrison, a Cromwellian army officer and leader of the Fifth Monarchy Men.

The governing charter in 1835, which created the Newcastle-under-Lyme municipal borough, absorbed the previous borough created through the charters of 1590 and 1664.

Newcastle-under-Lyme's early economy was based around millinery, as well as silk and cotton mills. Later coal mining, brick manufacture, iron-casting and engineering rose to prominence. Fine red earthenware and soft-paste porcelain tableware were produced in Newcastle-under-Lyme at Samuel Bell's factory in Lower Street between 1724 and 1754, when production ceased. Manufacturing earthenware tiles continued at several locations within the borough, though, including Burslem where many of our Wase family ancestors lived and worked. The making of fine bone china was re-established in the borough in 1963 by Mayfair Pottery at Chesterton.

By the late-19th century, the old industries of the town had disappeared or shrunk to small proportions and had not been replaced by new ones. This is because Newcastle-under-Lyme had essentially become a dormitory town, housing large numbers of people whose places of work were to be found in the heavily industrialised areas on its eastern and northern boundaries.

Audley is a rural village approximately four miles north west of the town of Newcastle-under-Lyme in Staffordshire, and it is the centre of Audley Rural parish.

The first mention of Audley is in the *Domesday Book* of 1086, when it was called Aldidelege, when the lands were held by a Saxon called Gamel. At this time, the area was very sparsely populated, and because of its distance from the major towns of Stafford and Chester there was little outside contact. There was a medieval castle at Audley Castle Hill during the late 13th century but only a low earthwork remains of that.

Our earliest Pointons

I am not entirely sure which line of Pointons down to the Randle Pointon born in 1726 is our line, but the sequence I describe below seems to have been popularly adopted in many family trees and the most verifiable from my own investigations. The problem is the many repetitions and variations of similar names as well as gaps in the birth records. I must acknowledge and thank Sally Chapman who has been of great assistance in resolving the mysteries of our earliest Pointon heritage.

Ranalphus Poynton (1573-1625) was born in Norton le Moors, and married Jane Meare at St Bartholomew's in 1593. The Pointon family had a habit of adopting mother's maiden names as children's names and as a result the 'Meare' name recurs down the generations. Jane Meare's ancestors stem back to 1428 in Norton le Moors genealogy.

As far as I can ascertain, Ranalphus and Jane had six children: John (who died at a young age), Ranalphus (our ancestor), Mary, Meare, Jane and Ann.

I found a comment from one researcher who had come across an interesting document on the Norton in the Moors Rent Roll for the last day of May 1608, which mentions Randulph (there are many spelling variations of this name!) Poynton. The clip reads:

> Badyley
> Richard Meare and
> Randulph Poynton for the   ] xij s iiij d
> moyty of one Messuage called   ]
> the hall of Badyley and the   ] ij capons
> moytie of one cottage there
> John Meare for the other moyty   ] xij s iiijd
> of the said messuage Cottage   ]
> and landes thereto belongyinge   ] ij capons
>
> Randulph Poynton for an Acre of land
> in Haddfeild(?) als the ferme by lease] vj d

Norton in the Moors Rent Roll for 'the last day of May'
1608[ix]

There is a Baddeley Green now at Norton in the Moors. The 'capons' are hens. It is probable that Richard and John Meare were relatives of the Jane Meare married to Ranalphus Poynton.

The next generation in this genealogy was **Ranalphus (also known as Randall) Poynton** (1595-1650), again born in Norton le Moors. He married Joyse and had at least five children: Johannis (John) (our ancestor,) Meare (1624-?), Jane (1626-?), William (1629-?), and Ellin (1631-?). Again, all these birth records are part of the St. Bartholomew's church records.

His son, and our ancestor, **Johannis Poynton** (1622-c.1698) was born at Norton le Moors and his first marriage was to Mary Lane by whom he had one daughter, Anne. Mary died in 1663.

Johannis then married Frances Rose from Wolstanton in 1666, and they had at least four children: John (Johannis) (1666-1712),

Meare (1667-1734), Richardus (1669-?) and Hezekiah (1674-1674).

The years of Johannis' generation were those of the Norman invasion, and William the Conqueror waged a number of savage campaigns to subjugate northern England, where the presence of the last Wessex claimant, Edgar Ætheling, had encouraged Anglo-Danish rebellions. For families such as the Poyntons, the period leading up to 1670 would have been terrifying as the Normans set out to burn, loot and terrify across the countryside, in campaigns known as the 'harrying'. While the worst affected were Yorkshire and North Riding, the impacts of food shortages and displacements were felt right across northern England. After the conquest, Norton in the Moors was given to the Norman Robert de Stafford.

The next generation is popularly believed to have been his second son, **Meare Pointon** (1667-1734), born at Norton-le-Moors, although this connection is a little shaky. Meare married Jane Mellor and their children, all born in Norton in the Moors, were:

- Jane (1692-?)
- Joyce (1697-?)
- Randulph Poynton (b.1703): If this was the Randulph who later married Hannah, and fathered at least four children: Sarah, Randulph, Hannah and Margareta, then this is our line. However, it is possible that this Randulph also died in 1703, soon after birth.
- Phillip (1708-1759)
- Mary (1713-?)
- William (1716-1716).

Meare's wife Jane's family has been traced back as far as the early 1500s. Jane's great, great Grandparents were Thomas and Alice Bentley from the ancient village of Caverswall, about seven miles south-west of Newcastle-under-Lyme. Listed in the *Doomsday Book*, 1086, Caverswall has its very own moated medieval castle that dates back to 1275. There was a large branch of the Bentley family in nearby Kingsley as well as in Caverswall. Jane's grandmother, Mary Bentley, married Thomas Mellor (1614-1705), also from Caverswall, and a member of a large extended family in the village.

Google Earth image of the moated castle at Caverswall

As mentioned above, it is also possible that not Meare, but **John Poynton** (who may even have been Meare's brother), was our ancestor. This John was married to Hannah and had a son Randulph who was born in 1699 at Norton in the Moors.

Both sons Randulph have been credited with having married 'Hannah', and having had four children (for whom there are birth records), the first two at Audley, and the second two at Wolstanton:

- Sarah (1722)
- Randle (1726)
- Hannah (1729)
- Margaret (1731)

So, there are two possible Randulphs who could be our ancestors at this stage: Randulph son of Meare, b.1703, or Randulph son of John, b.1699. As stated above, the Meare lineage seems to have been popularly adopted, but there are still some significant questions. Both lines have been linked to the son Randle (born 1726).

Randle Pointon (1726-c. 1787)

Randle was born at Audley, Newcastle and he married Sarah Whittell (1728-1805), in July 1744 at Wolstanton, Staffordshire. They had five children that I know of:

- John Pointon (1745-1841?)
- Elijah Pointon (1747-1750)
- Ann Pointon (1750 -1805?)
- Sarah Pointon (1752-?)
- Randle Pointon (1755-1840) (our ancestor).

Randle died at Burslem, only a few miles from Norton le Moors. Burslem is one of the more famous villages which produced Staffordshire pottery – see the Wase family chapter.

The spelling Pointon with an 'i' rather than a 'y' began to firm up at about this time, as did the name 'Randle'.

Randle Pointon (1755-1840)

This Randle was born at Wolstanton, again only a few miles from Norton-le-Moors. It appears that this family lived at Audley, for that is where most of their children were born. He married Jane Dale (1762-1841), and they had a least eight children:

- Abel Pointon (1779-1833)
- Hannah Henshall (born Pointon) (1781-1842): married Thomas Henshall in 1806
- Charlotte Sprowson (born Pointon) (1784-1853)
- Randle Pointon (1785-1830): married Hannah Hilditch at Audley in 1815 – William Pointon was a witness; they had five children. Hannah remarried in 1834 to John Bettely (1811-?) a coal miner 10 years younger than she
- Elijah Pointon (1787-?)
- Thomas Pointon (1790-1815): married Jane Darlington – they had only one child, Randle.
- John Pointon (1793-1833): married Amy Hilditch; Amy married Samuel Shepley in 1838 and in the 1841 census for Audley, all in the same street, were Jane Darlington with her son Randle Pointon 25 paviour; Joseph Pointon 15, collier; Jane Pointon 75; also an Abel Darlington and family; also a Thomas Darlington and family; Amy died in Fenton in 1867
- William Pointon (1794-1795): died in infancy
- **William Pointon** (1797-1851): our ancestor, married Hannah Wilson.

Randle died Wolstanton and is buried at Audley St James the Great Churchyard, which appears to have a very large gravesite attached to it. There has been a church on this site for over 1,000 years.

Jane died a year later and is buried in the same cemetery. In the 1841 census she was listed as living in Audley with her son Thomas' wife Jane Darlington and her son Randle, as well as a Joseph Pointon aged 15, who may have been her grandson.

William Pointon (1797-1851)

William was born at Audley, and married Hannah Wilson (1800-1875), also from Audley. There are several variations of his birth date, with 1794, 1797 and 1800 featuring regularly. He is listed as aged 54 in the 1851 census, which would make his birth year 1797, so this would seem to be the most likely. I am reasonably sure that Randle and Jane had two sons called William: one born in 1794 who died a year later, and then they used the name again (as was a common practice) for the next son and our ancestor, born in 1797.

Hannah's family came from Audley, with her grandfather Thomas having been the owner of the messauges (house and outer buildings) of Butter Farm which he left to his widowed daughter-in-law and grandsons in his will. His daughter-in-law Charity's maiden name had been Butter, so it is likely he was returning the farm to its original owners. There is still a Butter Green in Audley.

It is probable that earlier generations of the Wilson family lived in Wybunbury, Cheshire.

William Pointon and Hannah Wilson – marriage record

William and Hannah had at least six children:

- Charles Pointon (1819-c1863): a paviour, Charles married Mary Hand in 1841, lived in Newcastle-under-Lyme and had about eight children
- **William Pointon** (1820-1909): our ancestor, see below
- Mary Ann Pointon (1822-1883): Mary was at the family home in Bath Street with her parents, as well as brothers Charles and William in 1841. She married William Roberts in 1842 and was living in a de facto relationship with her later second husband in 1861. She married Charles Stockley in Wolstanton 1864 and lived there until her death in 1883. Her daughter Mary married Thomas Kitteridge, who had been lodging with her grandmother, Hannah Wilson, in 1865.
- Eliza Pointon (1827-1828): Eliza died in infancy.

William's occupation as stated on his son's birth certificate, was paviour (paver) and this seems to have been something of a family tradition.

One census record for 1841 has a William Pointon living in Burslem with his daughter Eliza, and his occupation is listed as 'earthenware xx [illegible]'. The age is about right to make the year of birth 1797, but I believe Eliza had died in infancy, so this is probably a different William.

The more likely 1841 census record for the Pointon family has them at Bath Street with William (a paviour) and Hannah both listed as aged 40, and children Charles, William and Mary at home. But this puts William's birth date as 1800.

The 1841 census was the very first England census where names were recorded, and mistakes and duplications were sure to occur. Ages of people in this census were usually rounded down to the nearest five years, which could explain the age discrepancies for

William. Enumeration forms were distributed to all households a couple of days before census night and the completed forms were collected the next day. If the head of the house was illiterate, or had any problems completing the form, the enumerator would assist as much as necessary, and this may well have been the case with Pointons. All the details from the individual forms were later sorted and copied into enumerators' books, and this may have the source of some additional errors.

There are also a few other records which possibly relate to our William. A William Pointon was found not guilty of larceny in the Staffordshire Court during Lent 1817. Several Pointons were tried for larceny, among other crimes, in a surprisingly long list of Pointons in the Staffordshire criminal registers.

Hannah Wilson[x]

Our William Pointon family lived for many years in Bath Street in Newcastle under Lyme. In 1851 he and Hannah were there without children but with two grandchildren, Mary and Emma Roberts.

In his will dated the eighteenth day of February 1843, William stated that he was a paviour of Newcastle under Lyme. The bulk of his estate, apart from two dwelling houses, was left to his 'dear wife', Hannah Pointon. Sons Charles and William benefited from the will. His daughter Mary Anne Roberts, then wife of William Roberts, and her daughter Mary were also mentioned. His dwelling houses at Hougher Wall in Audley and Hick Street in Newcastle-under-Lyme were left to Hannah, Charles and William.

William was buried at Newcastle-under-Lyme. Hannah continued to live at Bath Street and in 1861 had several lodgers. She was still there in 1871, along with her brother John, and died in 1875.

William Pointon (1820-1909)

This is the member of the Pointon family who came with his family to Australia on the Prince Consort in 1862 arriving in Moreton Bay Qld.

William Pointon[xi]

Born 18 October 1820 at Audley Staffordshire, William married Mary Wase on 21 March 1843 in the Burslem parish church. At the time, he was living at Burslem; she at Newcastle Street, and like his father his occupation was paviour.

The reason given for their emigration to Australia was the continued distress in the manufacturing districts, and they departed from Liverpool on 2 August 1862, among 102 passengers. The ship picked up a further 309 Passengers from Queenstown, in Cork, Ireland.

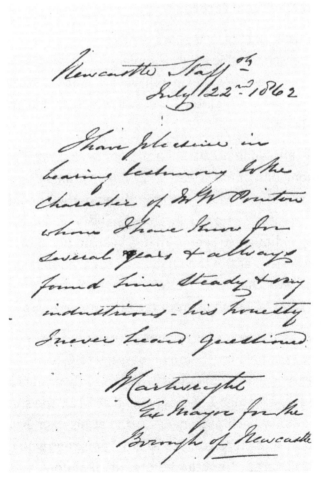

Reference from the former Mayor of Newcastle[xii]

The passenger list listed the following members of the Pointon family:

- William Pointon 41, labourer
- Mary Pointon 41, wife
- George Pointon, 18, labourer
- William Pointon, 16, labourer
- Henry Pointon, 14, labourer
- Abel Pointon, 8, child (our ancestor)
- Chas Pointon, 6, child
- Alfred Pointon, 2, child.

This ship was one of the Black Ball Line which was regularly bringing passenger ships full of emigrants to Australia. On this voyage three people died on the voyage and there were four births, however the Pointons were unaffected. The route took them via Tasmania.

The family arrived in Brisbane on the *Prince Consort* 3 November 1862, among one of four vessels carrying migrants that arrived in Moreton Bay in one week – a total of about 1500 people. At the time the greatest demand in Queensland was for agricultural labourers, although it seems that a restructuring of the land-allocation system at the time had been totally botched, resulting in an angry exchange of letters between AW Manning (PU Secretary) and AC Kemball, from the Brisbane Immigration office.

Originally the land order system provided that every adult immigrant who paid for their own passage to Queensland was to be granted a land order for 18 acres, and after two years residence in the colony, a further 12 acres (valued at £12). The ship owners received £18 for each passenger carried at his own expense and assisted passages were granted to any immigrant who could not pay the full fare. The year before the Pointons travelled to Australia, Mr Henry Jordan, a former member of the Queensland

Parliament, was appointed as Emigration Agent in England, operating from London. This was at the time when the outbreak of the American Civil War had prevented cotton from being shipped from the southern states to Britain, causing unemployment and distress among the Lancashire cotton workers – more than 2000 cotton mills had closed. Under the guidance of Mr Jordan, over 1700 of these starving families were brought to Queensland by the Black Ball Line.

After arriving at Australia, the Pointon family settled near Doughboy, and were apparently living near the White family.

The following newspaper article shows that the Pointons were all members of the Masons:

DOUGHBOY.

A CORRESPONDENT writes on February 5 :— the weather is still unsettled, but the crops as a whole look well. There has been some talk about getting a bridge across the creek, and opening a road into Bulimba ferry, which would be a great boon to the settlers on this side of the creek. Temperance is spreading in this locality. The usual weekly meeting of the Pioneer Lodge, No. 12, Good Templars, was held on the 30th ultimo, when the following officers were installed for the ensuing quarter by the L.D. :—George Pointon, P.W.C.T. ; James Gibson, W.C.T. ; Leonard Stemp, W.V.T. ; D. C. Mullin, W.S. ; Jessie Gibson, W.C. ; John Woodgate, W.F.S. ; Wm. Gibson, W.T. ; Abel Pointon, W.M. ; John M'Donald, W.O.G. ; B. Preston, W.I.G. ; C. Gibson, W.A.S. ; Charles Pointon, W.D.M.; Sister Margaret Gibson, W.R.H.S. ; Sister Matilda Stemp, W.L.H.S. There are twenty members on the roll of this lodge, not so bad for a small place like this.

Brisbane Courier Mail, 9 February 1873

William's eldest son, **George Wilson Pointon** (1844-1930) married Mary Morse (aged 18) not long after they arrived. George was a prison warden at St Helena from 11 November 1875 – 16 February 1877, and this information was among my great Grandfather Abel Pointon's records. He began as a paviour in England, as that was his occupation on the 1861 census. After leaving St Helena, he resumed the occupation of stonemason and, for several years, was in partnership with David Tweedy, though that dissolved in 1907. After that, he operated as a private contractor in the Brisbane area.

George and Mary had the following children:

- Eliza Jessie Pointon (1874–1928)
- Charles Alfred Pointon (1876–1954)
- George Wilson Pointon (1878–1973)
- Louis Francis Pointon (1880–1883)
- Mary Adelaide Pointon (1882– 1949)
- Lavina Rose Pointon (1884–1970)
- Violet Ellen Pointon (1887–1955)
- James Henry Pointon (1890–1944)
- William Albert Pointon (1892–1984)
- Lydia Naomi Pointon (1895–1996).

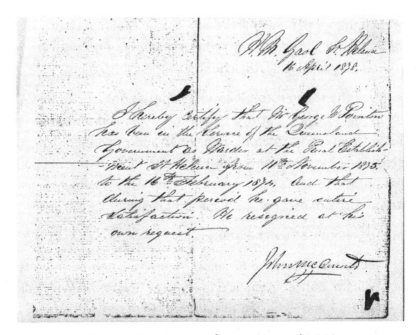

George Pointon – reference issued 1878

St Helena is in Moreton Bay and 5km from the mouth of the Brisbane River. It functioned as a high-security colonial prison from 1867. The overcrowding in Brisbane's jails resulted in the conversion of the buildings, originally intended to be a quarantine station, into accommodation for prisoners. Prison labour was used for all activities on the island, from the construction of buildings and roadways to growing, processing and cooking food.

The first few years were devoted to the construction of two cellblocks, a kitchen, bakehouse, hospital, underground tanks, stables, boathouse, storehouse, jetty and a superintendent's home. In 1869, a lime kiln and sugar mill were added. Sugarcane growing and processing kept prisoners busy until the workshops were established enough to take over as the main source of work on the island.

The St Helena Island penal establishment, at one stage of its operation, was considered to be the best prison of its kind in the world. It had prize Ayrshire dairy cattle that constantly won awards at the RNA show and the island's olive groves yielded prize-winning oil in Italy, the country of their origin.

The life of the island rotated around supervision of prisoners – as seen in the constant patrols, barred windows and leg irons. This constant regulation of work, behaviour and movement was the essence of 19th century prison life. Although few people could swim in those days and shark-feeding was instigated as a deterrent, risk of escape was a constant reality.

Among William's other children:

- **William Pointon** (1846-1922): Aged 16 when he migrated, William married Anna Maria Flynn at Grafton NSW. He died aged 59 and is buried at Balmoral Cemetery, Brisbane. He had been living at Lytton Road, Woolloongabba and was a labourer. Their children were: George Wilson (drowned in Norman Creek aged 6); William (died aged 9); John and Frank.
- **Harry/Henry Pointon** (1848-1868): Harry was 14 when the family migrated and died aged 20 (drowned).
- **Abel Pointon** (1853-1921): our ancestor, see below.
- **Charles Pointon** (1856-1913): Charles was 5 when the family migrated and he married Elizabeth 'Lilley' White – sister of my Great Grandmother, Alice White. Their children were: Ralph Gustavus (died aged 2); Adelaide (died as infant); Elizabeth Daisy (died aged 7); Alice Evelyn; Ruby; Mary Wase (Molly); Nellie (died in infancy); Charles, Joseph William; and Isabel Catherine. They lived at Hereford Hills, near Kilcoy.
- **Alfred Pointon** (1861-1938): A baby when the family migrated, he married Sarah McLean at Stony Creek Qld in 1884. Their children were: Bertha Elizabeth; Arthur; May; Ethel; Archie; Eva; Lillie; Violet; Hilda; and Donald. In 1903 Alfred was a farmer (manager) at Yedna, a sheep station

near Kilcoy, and was still there in 1913. My mother records that he took up much land in the Kilcoy district and learned Aboriginal language and skills including bark-pulling and tree climbing. He also became a taxidermist and snake charmer – and was bitten by a death adder in 1927. He took over Hereford Hills from his brother Charles. He died at Kilcoy in 1938.

In 1876 there is a record of an application by William Pointon of Wararba applying for a certificate under the Crown Lands Alienation Act. By 1922 William owned Hill Farm in the Woodford District and later Big Hill, Caboolture.

The William Pointon family later lived at Annie Street, New Farm, not far from the Brisbane River. William and Mary were listed as living there with son George on the 1905 electoral rolls. William died aged 89 on 9 August 1909 and is buried in the Lutwyche Cemetery in Brisbane, along with his wife Mary who had died in 1902.

George, William, Alfred, sitting Abel, Charles

Abel Pointon (1853-1921)

Our ancestor, Abel, born in Newcastle-under-Lyme was eight years old when the family arrived in 1862. He took up his father's trade as a master paviour and married Alice White (1861-1933), the eldest daughter of Joseph White of Doughboy Creek, at Bunya – see separate chapter on the White family. They had eight children, including my Grandmother, Alice Ivy Pointon.

Abel and his siblings were educated at a private school and, from the age of 11, he worked for Louis Hope in a sugar mill at Cleveland (now a suburb of Brisbane, and was probably the same place of work as Joseph White), from 1864-67.

Then he returned to work at Hill Farm, owned by his father, from 1867-74. In 1878 he and brother Charles bought 'Hereford Hills' on the Brisbane River at Hopetoun (now Kilcoy) under firm of A&C Pointon and it was here that they married their brides in 1879. Abel married Alice White on 9 July 1879 in a joint ceremony with Alice's sister Elizabeth Ann who married Abel's brother Charles at 'Bunya Farm', Upper Strathpine.

In 1888 Abel took up Gordon Brook, a property in South Burnett, and his partnership with his brother was dissolved in 1899. Abel Pointon retained Gordon Brook and his brother Hereford Hills. We have many photos of the family life at Gordon Brook, where they lived until it was sold in 1907. When he took over Gordon Brook, he built a new homestead in 1901 to replace the original shingle roof cottage on the property.

The Pointon family at Gordon Brook

About the same time as Gordon Brook was selected by Abel Pointon, another property, 'Wyuna', was selected by Harry Youngman. The demand for land at this time prompted the Government of the day to halve the Taabinga Run, and 151 square miles were resumed in 1886. The resumption included Wooroolin and Gordon Brook down as far as Home Creek. In 1887, Arthur

Youngman bought Taabinga Station and some years later, acquired Kingaroy Paddock from the Markwells.[16] The Youngman family continued a close association with the Lee family.

Percy, Amy, Gladys, Spot, Maude and Ivy Pointon, taken at Gordon Brook in 1896.[xiii]

Abel continued to acquire property during this time. In 1895 he purchased Lilyvale Station on the Dawson River and sold it about three years later.

Lilyvale and the nearby town of Clermont had been the site of a disastrous flood in January 1870, caused by the overflowing of Sandy Creek and carrying away houses, furniture and fences. In an hour there was nearly five feet of water over the town and, in some places, the current flowed at a rate of about eight miles per

---

[16] From Land Settlement in the South Burnett https://espace.library.uq.edu.au

hour. Some people took refuge in trees, and others on the tops of houses. By 9.00am the following day, the water had completely subsided. Nearly all the outbuildings in the town were swept away, and very little fencing was left standing. The total amount of damage sustained was estimated at £10,000. Business was completely paralysed. Five lives were lost at Peak Downs Station and Capella, and four children were drowned at Lilyvale. On the Wolfang Station, six to eight thousand sheep were lost and all the dams and miles of fencing washed away. In all, 15 lives were lost – six children, three women, and six men.

Abel and Alice Pointon 1888[xiv]

Abel also bought Wyuna Station, South Burnett in 1905 and took his son Albert Pointon in as a partner under firm of Al & A Pointon.

In 1907, aged 54, he sold Gordon Brook and made his home in Brisbane. A newspaper article in August of that year mentioned that he had been in town for two months undergoing medical treatment, so it is assumed that he left the station for health reasons. But even then, he continued to buy property and, in

1908, he bought Catunga Station in the Mitchell district, selling it a year later.

In Brisbane, the Pointons were prominent citizens with their activities frequently reported in the social pages of the newspapers – even to the extent of not being at home. In July 1913, *The Brisbane Courier* reported: "Mrs Abel Pointon, Dangore, Hamilton, will not be at home to-day." Most reports, however, related to Abel's yachting activities.

Abel really was a prominent pastoralist and citizen. He was a strong Nationalist and member of the Queensland National Association (forerunner of the National Party) and was made a life member of the Kingaroy Agricultural Pastoral Industry. He was also a keen boating enthusiast (owning a yacht, 'Alouette'), as well as fisherman and gardener. When he died his estate was valued at about £12000, close to $175,000 today.

WHO'S WHO IN AUSTRALIA.

ABEL POINTON, J.P.
Grazier
"Dangore," Langside Road, Hamilton, Brisbane

Abel Pointon's image from Who's Who in Australia, 1927[xv]

His home address in Brisbane was Dangore, Langside Road, Hamilton, Brisbane, and even today this is a very wealthy area, with 1 Langside Road selling for $2,675,000 in 2019. Dangore was first built by Wilfred Iliff in 1902 and today is a heritage property.

Family photo of Dangore, Hamilton[xvi]

26 Langside Road, Hamilton, today[xvii]

After WW1, the remaining family moved to a new 'Dangore', at 26 Sefton Avenue, Clayfield where their daughter Maude lived till 1959. Alice died there in 1933. Today this property is valued at $2.5m.

Abel is featured at the Stockman's Hall of Fame in Longreach, with information contributed by his granddaughter Shirley Webster (whom my Mother frequently mentioned).

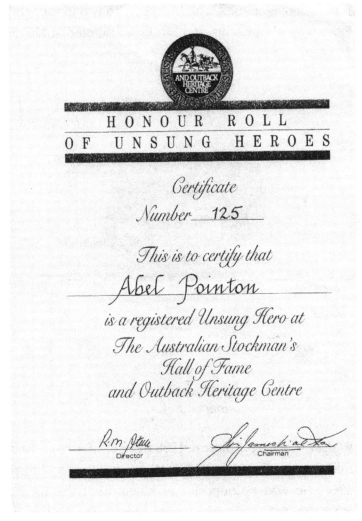

Abel Pointon – Stockman's Hall of Fame Certificate

Abel Pointon passed away on 28 April 1921 and Alice on 12 August 1933. A family plot is located at Dutton Park Cemetery, near the main entrance.

Children of Abel and Alice Pointon

- **Albert Leonard Pointon** (1880-1952): married Florence Kendall in 1911. Their early years were spent at Nanango. In 1924, the family was living at Manumbar station, which Albert managed for Alonzo Sparkes. They had four children: Florence, John, Cecilie and Marjorie. He died at Kingaroy in 1952.

Albert Pointon[xviii]

- **Walter Herbert Pointon** (1881-1966): Born at Hereford Hills, he married Margaret Wittkop, and died at Kingaroy in 1966. He was a Councillor at Kingaroy at the time of his marriage. Sally Chapman wrote that Herb (Walter Herbert Pointon) purchased Wywurri at Kingaroy, Queensland in the early 1920's. It was part of the original Gordon Brook and Wyuna holdings. It is said that Herb was always willing to give a helping hand to his neighbour and worked tirelessly to bring the school to the area. Their children were: Lorne, Ronald Bruce, Heather, Jean and Stuart.

Walter Herbert Pointon[xix]

Herb Pointon[xx]

- **Ida Maud Pointon (1884-1960):** Ida was born at Hereford Hills, Kilcoy. My Mother frequently referred to 'Aunty Maud', who never married and was a favourite Aunt of the family. In her early years she lived at Dangore, Hamilton. Like her sister, Ivy, her social life and activities were well documented in the Brisbane social pages.

For example an article in April 1934 read:

> *"On her arrival the Lady Mayoress was presented with a Victorian posy of golden-tinted roses and at the tea table her position was marked by a hand-painted place card and spray of artificial flowers made entirely from wool by Miss Maud Pointon."*

She lived in the family home at Sefton Avenue after her parents died. It is possible that she also curated art exhibitions and sales, because in a brief article in 1940, there is reference made to a 1930 one-made art sale for Roy Parkinson in which 49 pictures were sold, and which was managed by Maud Pointon.

Ida Maud Pointon[xxi]

- **Amy Pointon (1885-1903):** Amy died in Brisbane of cancer after incurring an injury at boarding school, aged 18.

Amy Pointon[xxii]

- **Perin (Percy) Charles Pointon (1888-1967):** married Florence Hillcoat in July 1924.

  Percy Charles Pointon enlisted on 27 March 1915 in the 11th Light Horse Regiment, 2nd Reinforcement, Australian Imperial Force, with the rank of Private, Number 865, and was listed as 'returned injured' to Australia on 23 July 1919, after suffering a gunshot wound to the head. At the time of his enlistment, his occupation was shown as 'station manager'.

The Hillcoat family was well-known and from Gympie. Florence was the granddaughter of John and Catherine Hillcoat, daughter of their son Harold.

The Hillcoats were the owners of Wodonga Station from 1887 when it was transferred from the Meakin brothers to Catherine Ellen Hillcoat, wife of John William Hillcoat, manager of Hope Crushing Battery at nearby Black Snake Mineral Field. John Hillcoat's son Harold and his wife settled on the property and raised their family of five boys and four girls. The Hillcoats continued the practice of cheese making and dairying and the family lived in the original homestead until 1902, when they constructed the current homestead.

Percy Pointon[xxiii]

From about 1908 the Hillcoats ceased dairying and concentrated on raising beef cattle, supplementing their income by selling possum and kangaroo skins. However, the property reverted to dairying under Percy Pointon who lived there after marrying Florence. Percy died at Gympie in 1967. After he died, the property was sold to the Wodonga Pastoral Company and was used to raise beef cattle again.

- **Alice Ivy Lee (born Pointon) (1892-1974):** my grandmother – see below

- **Gladys Ethel Webb (born Pointon) (1894-1969):** Born at Gordon Brook, Gladys married William Webb, a wool classer, in 1921. William had been in the same regiment as Percy and Abel Pointon during WW1, and they were evidently close friends, which is probably how he came to meet Gladys. He also served in the Second World War and was a prisoner of war on the infamous Burma (also known as 'the death railway') railway 1942. They had four children: John, Judith, William and Shirley. In the 1930s they were graziers at Stuart River, Nanango, and then were on Cheshire Station, Alpha.

William Webb's WWII service is recorded by the ANZAC Day commemoration committee. After enlisting at Maryborough in 1941, he was allocated to the 3rd Reserve Motor Transport Company, which was part of the Australian 8th Division. William was suffering from a bout of malaria when the Japanese bombarded Singapore in 1942. He left his hospital bed in search of his division at the docks and, amid the confusion, found himself on a ship heading for Java. He was subsequently reported 'missing', but in fact was a prisoner of war, one of 22,000 Australians were captured defending Malaya, Singapore, and the Dutch East

Indies. He was sent to help build a horrifying railway to carry supplies between Thailand and Burma.

Working in entirely unbearable conditions, the allied prisoners not only had to contend with brutal treatment dished out by Japanese and Korean guards, but had to battle all manner of tropical diseases, lack of shelter, 16-hour workdays and a near-starvation diet. Webb's will to survive never wavered. He would creep out of camp at night and trade with local people for food. He was well aware of the consequences if caught, but knowing that extra food gave him a better chance of staying alive made it worth the risk.

The railway was completed in October 1943, and Webb was one of the 900 men deemed 'fit' who were taken by rail to Bangkok and Phnom Penh, then by boat down the Mekong River to Saigon in French Indochina, where they were held in a disused French Foreign Legion camp, in which conditions were much improved after the frequently deadly and cruel Burma railway experience.

They were moved, again, to Singapore, where they joined a British contingent and met up with ships that would transport them to Japan. They were in Singapore for four months, on meagre rations. Forced into the holds of two ships, they set sail towards Japan, when they were torpedoed by US submarines. The Japanese took to the lifeboats and left the prisoners to fend for themselves.

Bill jumped ship and managed to reach a mate on some bamboo poles, nearly drowning in the process. Exhausted, they found their way back to the ship, which was still afloat. With another group, they managed to build a raft and escaped the ship shortly before it sank.

Ignored by two Japanese ships, they were eventually rescued by a group of men in lifeboats. Bill's group decided to row to China, a distance of about 350km. Those who remained were believed machine-gunned by the Japanese, but Bill's group was rescued and taken to work in Japanese coalmines and shipyards for the rest of the war.

Webb was finally freed in September 1945 by the American Occupation Forces.[17]

William Webb's marriage to Gladys ended in divorce in 1951, after William had an affair, and a child, with his niece, Cecilie Pointon (Albert's daughter). William and Cecilie married in 1952 and had two children: Elizabeth and Penelope, as well as one baby who died at birth in 1950. William died in 1975.

Gladys lived in Brisbane until her death in 1969.

Their daughter Shirley became Shirley Webster and embarked on a great deal of family research, and was a regular correspondent with my mother.

- **Abel Sydney Pointon (1895-1959)**

Born at Gordon Brook, Abel Sydney Pointon was a stockman when he enlisted, along with his brother, with the 11th Australian Light Horse Regiment during the First World War and was awarded the Military Medal. He married Margaret Campbell in 1923 and had two sons, Garth and David. In the 1930s and '40s they were graziers at Dalby, and by the 1950s were living at Raby Bay, Cleveland. My mother records that he was a wool merchant, in partnership for a time with his

---

[17] Adapted from : *William Webb The Survivor* – ANZAC Day Commemoration Committee.html

brother-in-law, William Webb. The family lived at Cecil Plains.

Alice Pointon with Abel and Percy

Alice Ivy Lee (born Pointon) (1892-1974)

Alice Ivy Pointon (always known as 'Ivy') was the sixth child of Abel and Alice Pointon, born at Burlington Street, East Brisbane on 26 April 1892.

My memories of my grandmother are of a stern woman with straight black (greying) hair and a walking stick which, at times, she brandished as a child admonishment. I was always fascinated by the fact that she did not marry until 1930, when she was 38, which was unusually late in life for the times. I was also curious about her earlier life: the sparsity of family papers reveal very little. In a moment of inspiration, it occurred to me that being the daughter of a wealthy pastoralist, she may have appeared occasionally in the social pages, and here I unearthed a treasure

Jenny Kroonstuiver

trove of information that has revealed a very different side of my grandmother.

The first mention was at a dancing school ball in September 1906, when she would have been 14. It was reported as 'Miss Porter's Ball' and was held at the Technical College in South Brisbane. Danby House in Edmonstone Street was a dancing school conducted by Mrs Porter and her daughters.

Following is the delightful description:

> "The hall was very prettily decorated with palms, flags and bunting. The blind musicians, Miss D'Arcy and Mr Turner, played splendid music; their timing was perfect. The supper tables were ornamented with fancy baskets of choice flowers and roses, intermixed with draperies of silk. A very dainty super was served. Mrs Porter received her guests in a handsome black silk evening toilette, softened with chiffon and relieved with scarlet flowers on corsage; her sister Miss Amy Porter, also wore a pretty black costume, softened with frills of tucked net, and sprays of heliotrope flowers.
>
> "... During the evening two very handsome presentations were made to Miss Porter and her sisters. Mrs Weatherill, on behalf of the senior pupils, presented Miss Porter with a very handsome eight-day marble clock; and little Miss Blanch Curnow, for the junior students, presented a solid silver cut glass fruit dish and spoon. Two handsome fancy baskets of flowers tied with streamers were also given from the pupils by Mr Schofield and Master Pointon [probably Abel].

"... Several pretty dances were given by the pupils ... Minuet, by Misses Kitty Melton, Vida Morris, Alice Healey, Ivy Pointon, Eva Weatherill, Ida Northage, Gladys Pointon, May Wilkins, Annie Runnick, Agnes Simpson, Jeannie Williams, May O'Brien, all wearing very pretty pale blue and pink Empire gowns ..."

Post card from 17 year old Ivy Lee during a visit to the family property of Wyuna in 1909[xxiv]

Wyuna homestad[xxv]

Four years later, in 1910, Ivy Pointon is mentioned as having taken out third prize in 'best three pictures, any size, any subject, for amateurs under 18 years' in a Fine Arts Exhibition. Ivy appears to have been quite a talented artist, because a report later that year states that the Governor's wife, Lady MacGregor, at the end of a speech, was presented with an album containing "a number of pretty little sketches, including the work of Miss Ivy Pointon..."

This painting by Ivy Lee, held by Yvette Dawson, is the only known painting still surviving

Ivy is reported as successfully completing the Pittman shorthand theory examinations in 1911.

In 1912, at the age of 20, Ivy was a debutante at Mrs Sparke's dance, in Crescent Road, Hamilton. Her parents are listed among the invited guests. The dance seems to have been an elaborate affair, with Chinese lanterns in the garden, and catering by the Café Eschenhagen. Eschenhagen's – "the Rendezvous of the Fashionable" – was a renowned restaurant. To be seen there was the 'done thing' socially, and the catering business associated with it set a standard that won for it the personal patronage of every governor of Queensland, from Sir Henry Wylie Norman in 1889 to Sir William MacGregor in 1914.

> *"Miss Ivy Pointon (debutante) wore white charmeuse with overdress of pretty lace, and a band of crystal in her hair."*

As the nation entered the war in 1914, and two of her brothers enlisted, young Ivy turned her hand to supporting the war effort. She was frequently mentioned assisting the Mayoress with fundraising through 'flags and badges' stalls.

Ivy joined the Red Cross, and was elected treasurer of the Hamilton Society, a position she held for several years. The Mayoress of Hamilton was the President, and the group presided over a variety of creative fundraising activities, including a material distribution centre. In 1914, the Telegraph reported:

> *"... From material supplied by the central executive the following garments were cut out by the distributing committee, consisting of the Mayoress, Miss E. M. Walker and Miss Ivy Pointon. Pajamas, 78 pairs; sheets, 208; towels, 232; pillow-cases, 500; housewives [sic], 85; long sleeve shirts, 120; hospital shirts, 120; also from wool supplied a number of cardigan jackets, socks, balaclava caps and other knitted articles were made up..."*

Ivy was frequently mentioned as the organiser of various collection drives and appeared regularly in the newspaper in her role as treasurer, reporting sums raised or received.

A second organisation in which she was active was the Soldiers' Church of England Help Society. This was an organisation formed and run by the chaplain of St Luke's Anglican Church, and Ivy and her father were members from the beginning. A newspaper report in 1915 listed among the society's activities the organisation of concerts for the different camps, sewing for the men in the camps, visiting hospitals and relatives, and distribution of goods such as Christmas puddings. By 1916, Ivy was the 'literature secretary', organising the collection and distribution of books and magazines. She also led the organisation of events such as tea for the soldiers. By the end of its first year, the society had built a new hut at Fraser's camp, was organising chaplains, had opened 39 different branches of the organisation, was regularly organising soldiers' teas and concerts, and was running sewing parties as well as distributing books. Ivy was evidently working regularly in the organisation's office at St Luke's by then, because her request for assistance with the office duties was considered and approved.

By 1917, Ivy was also a member (and treasurer) of the committee of the 11th Light Horse Comforts Fund (the regiment of her two brothers) and in April 1917 helped organise a jumble sale and entertainment.

General social life seemed to start returning in late 1918, after the end of the war. By now Ivy was 26. She was reporting as attending a 'dainty tea' for Mrs L. M. Bond where they were entertained by the Thursday Waitresses.

Her mother Alice entertained the committee from the Hamilton Branch of the Red Cross at her home in September 1919 in honour of the retiring president, Mrs Russell, who was to be presented with a gift. In her speech, Mrs Russell "referred to the splendid war work of Miss Ivy Pointon and presented her with a beautiful carved photograph frame." Both gifts bore a silver plate, with small enamelled red cross, and were inscribed.

War work gave way to the social life of the 1920s, and Ivy continued to regularly feature in the social pages of the various Brisbane newspapers. These events seem to have involved the cream of Brisbane society and included events such as afternoon musical programs.

Ivy's charity work continued, and in 1920 she was reported as having helped organise a 'Peace Loan Dance' for the Toombul branch of the Queensland Women's Electoral League in aid of the bursary fund. A year later she was organising a concert in aid of the Tufnell Home and Orphanage and had conceived the novel idea of making the admission "a silver coin or a bottle of jam".

This was also the year her father, Abel, died.

She continued to raise funds for the 11th Light Horse Comforts Fund and organised a fete in 1922. That same year she helped organise Red Cross fundraising to pay off the home of a digger, Mr Farrell, who had been blinded during the war and who had recently purchased a home, with his wife and four children. This work continued to at least 1926, when she was reported as being an organiser of an ANZAC Day event.

By now it was becoming evident that most of her social set was married. In 1922 she attended a performance of *The White-Headed Boy* at His Majesty's Theatre and appears to have been one of the few mature single women in attendance.

She was secretary of the St Augustine's Ladies Guild in 1923 and was responsible for helping to organise the first monthly dances on the Hamilton Town Hall. Later in 1923 she was reported as having attended a display of fancy dancing by the pupils of the Misses Edith Barry and Rosetta Powell, again in the company of a range of dignitaries.

The following year, her expertise in gardening and flower arranging began to be reported. She came second for 'one croton' in the Hamilton Horticultural Society's Autumn show. In 1926 she came first for 12 cut flowers (gerberas) and second for a 'vase of gerberas arranged for effect'. Gerberas seemed to be her forte, because she won prizes again for gerberas in 1929. In that same year she was awarded a medallion which was later investigated by my mother. A letter from the Department of Primary Industries explained that the medallion was purchased pre-war from the Royal Horticultural Society in London and were awarded to members who did outstanding work during the year. Ivy Pointon was awarded a bronze medal for 157 points gained in the cut flower sections in 1929.

That same year she attended an engagement party for Dora Fuller at Lennon's Hotel. A year later she was reported at representing St Augustines, Hamilton, at an Anglican synod tea held at St Lukes, as well as attending a farewell tea for Miss Edna Mundell. The decorations seemed to follow the traditional style, although the dresses were very different to earlier years.

> "The decorations consisted of pink and white tulle puffings and pastel tinted stocks. Miss Mundell received her guests wearing a grey gaberdine frock, soutached with braid, and ornamented with gold buttons. Her grey hat harmonised with her costume."
> The Telegraph, Brisbane 23 September 1925.

By 1926, mahjong and bridge began to feature as social events and were the subject of a benefit event organised by the St Augustine's Ladies Guild – Ivy was both secretary and treasurer in that year. That same year Ivy attended a mahjong party at the home of Mrs James Cleeve. In December, she arranged another elaborate mahjong and bridge evening at the Hamilton Town Hall for the Ladies Guild. Usually, these events were fundraisers, such as the occasion held at the home of Mrs Herring in May 1927.

By this time, Ivy was 33 and there is no mention of her 'stepping out' or being in the company of any male. She was still living at the family home, and it is assumed that her charity work took up most of her time. She judged the cooking competition at an Anglican mission hall fete at Hendra in 1927, but high-society bridge and mahjong continued to feature regularly. In 1927 she was reported by the Queensland Figaro as attending a:

> "most successful bridge mahjong and tennis afternoon, which was held in the charming home and ground of Mrs RG Clarke, 'Clovelly' Hamilton. The three hostesses, knowing how much a personal touch counts, left no stone unturned to make their 'big effort' an unqualified success, and as there was little or no expense, the worthy object for which the funds for the function was in aid of (the Seamen's Institute) should receive a very welcome addition."

Tennis did not receive much mention in the social pages before this, but Ivy was evidently a reasonably accomplished player because in 1928 she won second prize in a tennis tournament organised in aid of Mr Eric Sparkes, the aquatic candidate in the Ugly Man Competition for the cancer campaign fund. Interestingly, this event was also attended by a player, 'Lee', which may be the first mention of an event that both she and her future husband, Fred, attended. He would have been recently widowed, and I can see the social set trying to get him involved in social events.

In 1929 she is reported as attending Gwendolyn Grant's exhibition of paintings at the Regent Building, and later a farewell tea for Mrs Caravasso at Rowe's Café.

The very last social event she is reported to have attended was a bridge afternoon in November 1929. This party was held at

Newstead House to assist the candidature of Mr George Rees, who was the bowler's nominee in the 'Prince of Sports' competition in connection with the limbless soldiers' appeal.

"Tables were arranged for play on the flag-enclosed verandahs, which command such a picturesque view of the river. The reception rooms were decked with roses and gerberas." (Brisbane Courier, 5 November 1929)

Three months later the following marriage notice appeared in the Brisbane Courier:

MARRIAGES.

LEE—POINTON.—At St. Augustine's, Hamilton, on 10th February, Fred. S. Lee, to Ivy, daughter of Mrs. A. Pointon, Sefton-avenue, Clayfield.

Ivy Pointon and Fred Lee – marriage notice

From the time of her marriage, Ivy seems to disappear from the social pages. This is understandable in part because she had three children in quick succession after she was married, and then a few years after that the family moved to Nanango.

Jenny Kroonstuiver

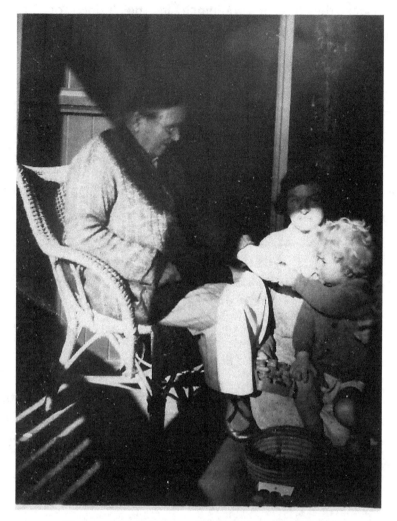

Three generations – Alice, Ivy and Nancy[xxvi]

Ivy's story continues in the Lee family chapter, as well as in Ruth's story.

The Wase family

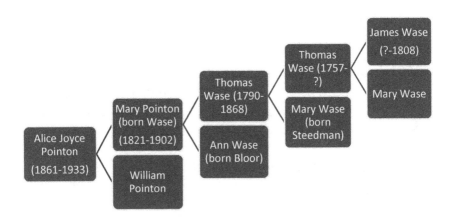

The surname 'Weise' was first found in Bavaria, where the name gained a significant reputation for its contribution to the emerging mediaeval society. It later became more prominent as many branches of the same house acquired distant estates and branches, some in foreign countries, always elevating their social status by their great contributions to society.

The Anglicised version of the name, 'Wase', is connected to our family through Mary Pointon, Alice Ivy Lee's Grandmother.

Our Wase ancestors originated in the Market Drayton ward in north eastern Shropshire.

Market Drayton itself is a market town close to the Cheshire and Staffordshire borders. It is on the River Tern and was formerly known as 'Drayton in Hales' (c. 1868) and earlier simply as 'Drayton' (c. 1695). Drayton is recorded in the *Domesday Book* as a manor in the hundred of Hodnet, and is listed as having a population of five households in 1086.

In 1245 King Henry III granted a charter for a weekly Wednesday market, giving the town its current name. The market is still held every Wednesday.

Nearby Blore Heath was the site of a battle in 1459 between the Houses of York and Lancaster during the Wars of the Roses.

The great fire of Drayton destroyed almost 70 per cent of the town in 1651. It was started at a bakery, and quickly spread through the timber buildings. The buttercross in the centre of the town still has a bell at the top for people to ring if there was ever another fire.

In later generations the Wase family gravitated towards Newcastle-under-Lyme.

James Wase (?-c 1808)

Details of our earliest known Wase ancestor James' birth are unknown, but it is believed that his wife's name was Mary, and they lived originally in Cheswardine, Market Drayton. They had at least seven children as listed below, and at the time of James' death in 1808 (Mary had died in 1779) were still living in Cheswardine. He was buried on 7 April 1808 at St. Swithun's Church (C of E), 8 High Street, Cheswardine, Market Drayton.

Cheswardine is a rural village and civil parish about five miles south east of Market Drayton. The name Cheswardine is probably derived from the Old English for 'cheese-producing settlement'.

Cheswardine was mentioned in the Domesday book, when the manor was held by Robert of Stafford, but is probably a much older settlement. The moat, earthworks and some buried ruins of Cheswardine Castle (built in the 13th century) were scheduled as a historical monument in 1976.

The parish church, dedicated to St Swithun, overlooks Cheswardine from the hill at the top of the village. This is at least the third church on this site and was rebuilt in 1887-1889. It is because of the records retained from this church that we are able to trace so many members of the Wase family.

Their children were:

- George Wase (1745-1825)
- James Wase (1749-1828)
- William Wase (1752 - ?)
- John Wase (1754-1804)
- **Thomas Wase** (born 1757 in Cheswardine, Shropshire), our ancestor
- Samuel Wase (1759-1850)
- Anne Wase (1761-?)
- Jane Wase (1764-1764)
- Mary Wase (1765-1768)
- Sarah Wase (1768-1856)
- Joseph Wase (1771-1837).

It is rare to find a surviving will from this era, but James's will does survive. Son Thomas, along with Thomas Butterton, was executor of will on 25 July 1808. The main beneficiaries were George Wase (son), Sarah Steedman (daughter), while the residual estate went to James Wase (son) and Samuel Wase (son).

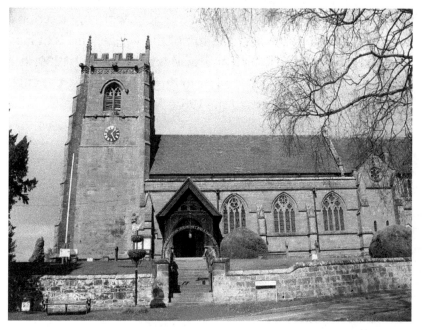

St Swithun's Church, Cheswardine, taken in 2011[xxvii]

Thomas Wase (1757-?)

The next ancestor was Thomas Wase, a joiner, born in Cheswardine in 1757. He was christened on 16 Jan 1757 in St. Swithun's Church. Thomas married Mary Steedman (1758-?) in 1787 at Whitmore – a village which lies between Market Drayton and Newcastle-under-Lyme.

It is possible that Mary was a relative of Thomas's brother-in-law, Abraham Steedman, who married his sister Sarah Wase in Stoke-on-Trent in 1805. The only child I definitely know of is their eldest son Thomas, born in 1790 in Tyrley, Cheswardine, and our ancestor. Some family trees have additional children.

Thomas' possible children, all born in Market Drayton:

- Mary (1789 - ?)
- **Thomas** (1790-1868), our ancestor
- Eleanor (1793 - ?)

- James (1795 - ?)
- Samuel (1797)
- Sarah (1797 -?)
- John (1801 - ?).

According to the Newcastle-under-Lyme poll books, in 1832 a Thomas Wase held a freehold shop in Bagnall Street Pirehill South, Newcastle under Lyme – though maybe this was his son.

Thomas Wase (1790-1868)

The next generation was also Thomas Wase, born in Market Drayton in 1790. He married Ann (also known as Mary Ann) Bloor (1802 – 1837) at Norton in the Moors in 1819. It was interesting that she signed her name as 'Blore', and that they were married at St Bartholomew's Church instead of the local church.

Thomas Wase and Ann Bloor, marriage record

I am grateful to the research undertaken by Ian Jones which assisted in the discovery of the additional information about Thomas Wase. There is a Deed of Assignment from 1826, published in the *Staffordshire Advertiser,* stating: "Legal notice: Thomas Wase, joiner and cabinet maker, assigns over all of his real and personal Estate to Mr. Robert Bull, Wine and Spirit Merchant, in trust for himself and all other of his Creditors who shall execute the same on or before 18th August". Thomas became a publican in about 1833. There is a record of him breaching licensing laws in 1836 as he was fined for keeping his house open during the hours of divine service on a Sunday. In 1839 he received a further fine for allowing drunkenness and other disorderly conduct in his house.

Thomas was also connected to a murder mystery. There is an interesting article in the *Staffordshire Advertiser* from 1834, where Thomas was called as the chief witness in the death of a young man named Walthew, a young man of 'respectable connections' who had been found near death in an out-house of the Shakespeare Inn and who subsequently died. Initially there had been no suspicion about the death, but a new police officer overheard a conversation and conducted an investigation which subsequently led to the arrest of Biddulf with Thomas Wase called as the chief witness. The rather salacious newspaper article stated that Thomas had evidently claimed that he was drinking a glass of gin at the Shakespeare when he heard a very great noise upstairs with bad language, and a man (presumably Walthew) had been flung down the stairs. Biddulf evidently told Thomas Wase he had tumbled down the stairs because he had been taking liberties with his daughter, and gave him a glass of gin to not say anything. The magistrates determined from the 'nervous excitement' of Thomas, plus evidence subsequently received which had determined him as being of 'unsound mind', that he was not competent to give evidence, at which point Biddulf was allowed to go free.

In the 1841 census, Thomas was already a widower, and was a publican living at Bath Street in Newcastle-under-Lyme. Living with him were Mary (20), Martha (15, a dressmaker), Sarah (12), Edward (10), Hannah (8). His wife, Ann, had died in 1837 at the age of 35. On her death certificate, Thomas is listed as being of the 'Swan with two necks'. There is still a 'Swan with two necks' restaurant in Nantwich Road, Blackbrook, but this is not the same pub. Thomas' pub was in Bath Street, the same street where he lived, and there was a joiner's shop behind, which makes sense because Thomas was originally a joiner. Bath Street runs between Salter's Lane and Marsh Street. Thomas' father's joinery shop in Bagnall Street was a short distance away.

Entry from the 1841 census

Their children were:

- **Mary Pointon (born Wase):** at Newcastle-under-Lyme, Staffordshire 1821, and our ancestor – see below.
- **Thomas Wase (1822-1830):** Thomas died as a young child.
- **Martha Wase (1826–after 1901):** In 1841 Martha was a dressmaker, living with the family at Bath Street. By 1851, she was a milliner and was living with her sister Mary at 17 Wick Street, Newcastle-under-Lyme. She most likely married Benjamin Jones, and iron puddler, in 1856. In 1861 they had one child (Herbert). By 1871, there was another child (Charles), but Martha was alone with the children at 15 Cotton Street and working as a milliner/dressmaker. They were in Bridge Street in 1881, and Benjamin was home again, by this time a ballast man; Arthur was a cabinet maker. All three were in Foden Street in 1881. Martha had

been widowed by 1901 and was still living with son Arthur, now married to Flora, and their daughter. There is no record of Martha after this.

- **Sarah Wase:** (1827-1843): born in Newcastle-under-Lyme. In 1841, Sarah was living with the family in Bath Street. It is possible that she died two years later.
- **Edmund Peel Wase** (1831-1875): In 1840 Edmund was a lodger, and a potter/presser, with Joseph Middleton at 126 Cobridge Street, Stoke upon Trent. In 1851 he was unmarried and a potter, living with his father at Stoke upon Trent. He was still living with his father in 1861 in Lyme Street, Newcastle. He died in 1875 aged 45. At the time of his death his occupation was potter's holloware presser and he was living at Union House (a workhouse), St. Giles.
- **Hannah Findler (born Wase)** (1832-1908): In 1841 she was living with her father in Bath Street. In 1851 she was a house servant in the house of Josiah Powell at 97 King Street, Burslem. In 1852, she married Thomas Findler and by 1861 was living at Fenton Flint Mill at Stoke-upon-Trent. Thomas was a flint miller, and they had two children, Emily and Thomas.

Ten years later, in 1871, Thomas was a labourer and they lived at 87 Sneyd Croft Street in Burslem; three more children (Hannah, John and Joseph) had been added. Things had improved in 1881, for Thomas was a potters' miller, as were sons Thomas and John, living at 225 Newport Lane, Burslem. In 1891 they had moved to Wigley's Terrace. By 1901 Hannah was a widow, living alone in Shelton Rd. She died in 1908. Thomas died in 1900.

If my interpretation of the following letter is correct, Thomas Findler and the rest of the family were separated by about 1895. This letter was among Abel Pointon's papers, and it took some time to track down who the various people were. I believe them to be the following:

o the writer, Hannah, is Hannah Findler's daughter

o 'Uncle and Aunt' are Mary and William Pointon

o 'Mother' is Hannah Findler (born Wase)

o the 'farther' in 'farthers bad doings' is Thomas Findler

o Mother's 'two unmarried sons' are her sons Thomas and John

o 'Uncle and Aunt Jones' are Martha and her husband Benjamin Jones

o 'sons John, Joseph' are the writer Hannah's sons.

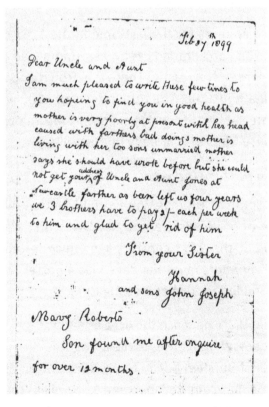

Mysterious letter from our family records

Thomas Findler died of acute bronchitis, aged 68, in 1900. At the time he was living at 59 Beeches Row, Sandyford, Tunstall (this thoroughfare no longer exists). This was the same address as his daughter Elizabeth Kinsey, who was present at his death, so there must have been some sort of reconciliation with his family. Elizabeth had married Albert Kinsey in 1894, but they do not appear in any census records.

- **Josiah Dale Wase** (1834-?): may well have died as a child, as he does not appear with his father in the 1841 census.

In 1851 Thomas Wase was still living in Bath Street but was once again a joiner and was living alone.

Thomas Wase appears for the last time in the 1861 census, aged 72, living with his son Edmund Peel Wase, unmarried and a potter, at 102 Lyme Street, Newcastle. There is a probate notice from the time of his death in 1868. The total effects of £100 were handled by his daughter Martha Jones as executor. Martha was probably chosen because Mary was already in Australia.

The Burslem pottery industry

It is through some of Thomas Wase's children that we have a link to the home of Staffordshire pottery. I was first alerted to this when looking at the 1841 census page which included Edmund Peel Wase. Every person on the page was a potter, which piqued my interest and led to further investigation.

The pottery industry began in the area as early as the 13th century with the Adams family the earliest identifiable potters. The Wedgewoods of Burslem began to produce pottery in the 1650s, by which time Burslem had become known as 'the mother of potteries'. By 1710 there were 35 potworks in Burslem, with more in surrounding villages, and the industry continued to grow. There is a family belief that one of the Pointons may have married a Wedgewood, but I have not been able to verify this.

By the late 18th century, the hilly area of North Staffordshire was the largest producer of ceramics in Britain, despite significant centres elsewhere. Large export markets took Staffordshire pottery around the world, especially in the 19th century.

In 1840, about the time Edmund Peel Wase joined the industry as an apprentice potter, there were 24 pottery works at Burslem. There was considerable increase in the business at this time as the coming of the railway increased distribution options. The main product was earthenware with a certain amount of vitrified ware and redware, but only four works were producing bone china.

Milling was a dusty, physical job and living and working conditions in the potteries were hazardous due to the pollution from all the hundreds of bottle kilns. Many of the workers died early from respiratory diseases and conditions.

The Wase family were based around Sambrook and Cheswardine, south of Market Drayton, which is on the main road from Shrewsbury to Newcastle-under-Lyme (all old established market towns).

The six towns (Stoke, Hanley, Fenton, Longton, Burslem and Tunstall) grew up along a coal seam (twice as much coal as clay was needed to produce pots). As populations grew, a lot of farm labourers moved off the land into the industrial cities, which is probably why some of the Wase family to move to Newcastle and Stoke-on-Trent, which was formed by the amalgamation of the 'six towns' in 1910, although Newcastle remained separate.

Potteries active in the 19th century include Spode, Aynsley, Burleigh, Doulton, Dudson, Mintons, Moorcroft, Davenport, Twyford, and Wedgwood. Hundreds of companies produced all kinds of pottery, from tablewares and decorative pieces to industrial items. The main pottery types of earthenware, stoneware and porcelain were all made in large quantities, and the Staffordshire industry was a major innovator in developing new varieties of ceramic bodies such as bone china and jasperware, as well as pioneering transfer printing and other glazing and decorating techniques.

Production had begun to decline in the late 19th century, as other countries developed their industries, and declined steeply after World War II. Some production continues in the area, but at a fraction of the levels at the peak of the industry.

Mary Pointon (born Wase) (1821-1902)

Mary is the Wase family member who came with her family to Australia on the *Prince Consort* in 1862, arriving in Moreton Bay Qld.

Mary was born at Newcastle-under-Lyme in 1821 and was the eldest of the Wase children. Her mother died when she was just 15, so it is quite likely that responsibility for management of the household and younger children fell to her from this time. In the 1841 census she was aged 20, and still at home in Bath Street with her family.

Her future husband's parents lived just two doors away, so it is likely that this is where she met William Pointon, a paviour, who at this time was living in nearby Burslem. They married in 1843.

William Pointon and Mary Wase - marriage record

According to the 1851 census they were living in Newcastle-under-Lyme, by which time three of their children had been born.

Entry from the 1851 census

By the 1861 census, our ancestor Abel, as well as Charles and Alfred had been added to the family and they were living at 154 Earl Street.

Earl Street today – Google Earth image

A year later the whole family migrated to Australia, and Mary's story continues in the Pointon chapter.

Mary died in 1902, at 'Big Hill' Woodford, Queensland, and is buried in the Lutwyche Cemetery.

The White family

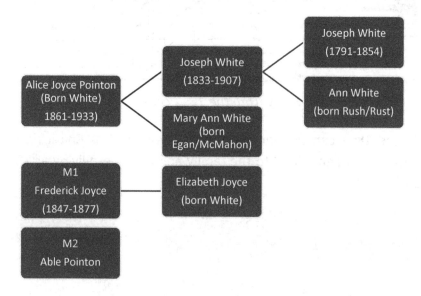

Trying to identify specific people in England with a name like 'White' is like trying to isolate a drop in a puddle. In addition, some members of this family seem to have changed names for convenience at times, so identifying them has been doubly challenging. The best way is to start with the definite and then gradually eliminate the outliers and inconsistencies. So, the real 'knowns' are my great-great-grandparents, Joseph White and Mary Ann McMahon, who married in Mt Gambier on 13 November 1859. Family details earlier than that have been developed through a process of elimination.

Was this Joseph White the son of the Joseph White from Conington, as described below? This has been one of the mysteries of our heritage. I have vacillated from 'yes' to 'no' many times in writing this book, even to the point of persuading one genealogist to adjust his family tree. I settled on the 'yes' side, mainly because even though various family members arrived and initially worked in different states, they all ended up at Hemmant, just out of Brisbane, and I suspect this was more than a coincidence. The second reason is because most of our own family trees have suggested they are all connected, although there is minimal evidence.

Joseph White (1791-1854)

We know from his son's Mt Gambier marriage certificate that this man's name was Joseph White. Papers from my mother's records, which include a White family tree, call him 'Joseph' and state that he came from Cambridge in England, possibly 'Carrington', since his son was born there. However, there is no Carrington in Cambridgeshire (that I can find) and other records suggest 'Conington', so I have gone with that, especially as he most likely died in Conington.

Conington is an English village and civil parish in the Cambridgeshire, about 10 km south of Peterborough. The area is mostly pasture, and Conington Fen, which occupies a large part of the eastern side of the parish, is now mostly drained and cultivated.

The Fens, also known as the Fenlands, is a coastal plain in eastern England. This naturally marshy region supports a rich ecology and numerous species and helps absorb storms. Most of the fens were drained centuries ago, resulting in a flat, dry, low-lying agricultural region supported by a system of drainage channels and human-made rivers (dykes and drains) and automated pumping stations.

The farms during the 17th century were mostly pasture, but after the purchase of the manor by Sir John Heathcote the arable land was increased. In 1751 a good deal of land was planted with woad[18]. In 1800 there were 270 acres of arable land, which by 1838, and the time of Joseph, had fallen to 250 acres, and by 1921 had increased to about 600 acres, which tended to increase the size of farms.

The somewhat scattered village lies along the lane called Conington Lane, which leads to the church and Conington Castle or Manor House. The Crown and Woolpack, formerly the Woolpack Inn, on Ermine Street, is said to have been frequented by Dick Turpin (an English highwayman whose exploits were romanticised following his execution in York for horse theft in 1739). The well-known episode of Turpin putting on the shoes of his horse the wrong way in order to mislead his pursuers is said to have taken place here.

For Joseph White, the most likely birth date is 1791, calculated from the entry in the 1841 census.

There is a marriage record between Joseph White and Anne 'Rust' – which could very possibly have been 'Rush' (no image was available, just a transcription) – for 10 October 1819 at Fen Drayton, which certainly fits. It is likely that Anne was born in 1794 in nearby Little Eversden, Cambridgeshire.

In the 1841 census the White family was living in High Street, Conington. Joseph is listed as aged 50, which puts his birth date around 1791. There is no sign of wife Anne (who died in 1837), nor of daughters Elizabeth and Lydia (who could have been in service), but the age of son Joseph does seem fairly close to our ancestor's age (bearing in mind that ages given in the 1841 census were often approximated).

---

[18] Woad is a yellow-flowered European plant of the cabbage family. It was formerly widely grown in Britain as a source of blue dye, which was extracted from the leaves after they had been dried, powdered, and fermented.

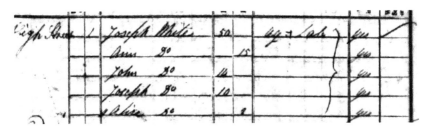

Entry from the 1841 census

If we look for the same family in the 1851 census, then the closest matches for son Joseph and daughter Alice are possibly living with the Joyce family at No 41 High Street. They were in the same street, so it is highly likely the families were related. In this entry the age of Joseph is about ten years older than our Joseph (if the recorded age is 30, but the translation says 20); and the Alice (visitor) could have been his sister.

Name and Surname of each Person who abode in the house, on the Night of the 30th March, 1851	Relation to Head of Family	Condition	Age of		Rank, Profession, or Occupation
			Males	Females	
Thomas Joyce	Son		3		
Frederick White	Son in law		6		Scholar
Emma Joyce	Daur				
Alice Do	Do				
Joseph White	Lodger		30		Ag. Lab.
Alice Do	Visitor	U		18	

Entry from the 1851 census

It is possible that Joseph, the dad, had fallen on hard times, as I think I found him at No 10, aged 60, living as a lodger in the house of John Mason. He is listed as a 'pauper, works on road'. This may explain why his son and daughter are living with the Joyce family.

Entry from the 1851 census

Joseph and Ann had the following children:

- **Elizabeth Joyce (born White)** (1819-1913): see below.

- **Lydia White** (1820- after 1891): Born in Fen Stanton, in 1841 it is possible that, aged 20, she was a house servant in the home of Henry Wallis, a bookseller at Holy Trinity, near Peterborough, although this does seem a long way from her family home. She probably married agricultural labourer Richard Day at St Ives in 1838 and had four children. The family lived at Elsworth, although Richard had died by 1871. Lydia was still alive and living at the same address in 1891.

- **William White** (1823-1907): In 1851 and 1861 he was a journeyman lodging at the home of James Austin at St Ives. William married Susan Brickwood in 1861 at Fen Drayton and had at least two children. By 1871, Susan had died, he had become a shoemaker. His sister-in-law Lydia had moved in as housekeeper to his two daughters at Sheep Market, St Ives. They were still there in 1891. By 1901 he was an alms-house inmate at St Ives.

- **Anne White** (1824-1906): Anne was still with her father in High Street in 1841. She married John Brand, an agricultural labourer, in 1844, and they had at least twelve children and lived at Fen Stanton.

- **John William White** (1830-1909): He was in High Street in 1841. There is a marriage record for a John White who married Eleanor Barnett at Winwick, Huntingdon in 1854 – this is the next shire, so it is quite possible that this is the son John from the 1841 census. This would make sense as in 1851 there is a John White, aged 25 and an agricultural labourer, listed as a lodger with Elizabeth Marriott in Winwick at No 53. There was a Barnett family living at No 38.

- **Joseph White** (1830-1909) (this was our ancestor) See below.

- **Alice White** (1832-?) Alice was probably with the Joyce family in 1851. It is not known what happened to her after 1851.

Joseph most likely died 8 Dec 1854 in Conington, Cambridgeshire.

Elizabeth Jane White (1819-1913)

Although not our direct ancestor, it is worth writing about Elizabeth because she was the mother of my Great Grandmother Alice's first husband, Frederick Joyce, and because of the close relationship between the Joyce and White families.

Elizabeth was born on 22 August 1819 at Fen Drayton, Cambridgeshire, the daughter of Joseph White, and was quite possibly a sister to our ancestor, Joseph White. There are a few possibilities for her on the 1841 census, and it is most likely she was in service at that time, possibly in the house of John Osler in Haddenham, which is reasonably close to her home of Fen Drayton.

At the age of 28, she married John Joseph Joyce at the Conington Parish Church on 16 October 1847. John's father Thomas is shown as deceased, and Elizabeth's father Joseph White is shown as 'labourer'. Although the writing is unclear, it is likely that Elizabeth had been living at Fenstanton at the time of her marriage. Both Fen Drayton and Fenstanton are neighbouring villages to Conington, and are only about a mile apart.

Google Earth image of Fenstanton and surrounding villages

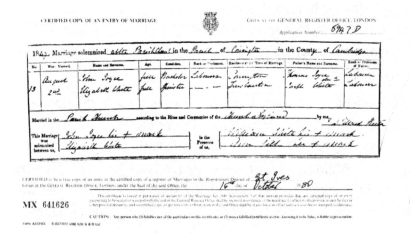

John Joyce and Elizabeth White, marriage record

By the census of 1851 their son Thomas (b 1848) and daughter Emma (1850) had been born. Another daughter, Alice was born in 1851, and son Alfred and daughter Elizabeth Ann were born in 1854.

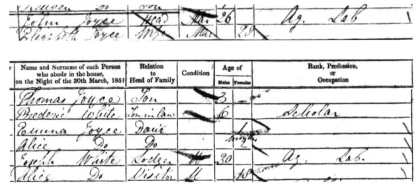

1851 census record – appeared across two pages

The 'Frederick White' on this document is a curious entry, and I cannot see how he can be a 'son-in-law' given the young age of John and Elizabeth. However, as many family trees list Elizabeth's son Fredrick John Joyce as having been born in 1843, and the age of this Frederick White is quite close, I can only surmise that Elizabeth gave birth to Frederick before she was married, and he was later adopted by her husband John Joyce.

On the 1861 census, the family was living in High Street Conington. By this time Frederick (16) is listed as John's son, and the other offspring and their ages were: Thomas (13), Emma (12), Alice (11), Alfred (8), Elizabeth Ann (6), John (4) and Susan (1). The two elder boys are listed as agricultural labourers, along with their father.

In 1871 the family was still in High Street, Conington. Frederick, Thomas and Emma had all left home. Alfred and John were agricultural labourers, Susan a 'scholar', and another son Joseph (9) who was a 'ploughboy', had been added to the family.

It was difficult to find them in the 1881 census. Son Thomas and his wife Hannah were lodgers at no 16 High Street, and they had 5 children. The Joyce family home in High Street was occupied by another family. It seems that they may have moved to Clayton and were living at 92 Cowgate Street. At home were Susan (21), Joseph

(19) a dairyman, granddaughter Emma (3) and grandson Errol (3m). I am sure these were Susan's children because they were still with her in 1891 in Little Horton, Bradford – by that time she was a weaver and Emma a spinner. Susan was living alone in Bradford as a 'worsted weaver' in 1901.

The Bradford textile industry had been steadily growing and by 1900, the number of mills was 350. Two-thirds of the country's wool production was processed in Bradford. From 1856, the law allowed children over the age of nine to work sixty hours per week, night or day, and Susan's daughter Emma, as well as many of her cousins, would have been among these children. A shocking statistic is that only 30 per cent of children born to textile workers reached the age of fifteen. Life expectancy in Bradford in the late 19th century was just over eighteen years, one of the lowest in the country.

Susan's mother, Elizabeth White, arrived in Brisbane on the *Merkara* in September 1885 – by this time Elizabeth was aged 65, and she is shown as a single passenger. However, her daughter Elizabeth Mitchell and her family were on the same ship. Her husband John had died in March 1885, before she departed. What a huge decision this must have been for Elizabeth. Newly widowed, considered quite elderly for the times, she left her home of a lifetime, many members of her extended family, and travelled to the other side of the world, not knowing what to expect.

Elizabeth died in June 1913, at the age of 98, at Woodford, a town in the Moreton Bay region of Queensland. Her obituary read:

DEATH OF AN OLD RESIDENT.

Mrs. Joyce, an old identity in this district, passed away at the residence of her son-in-law, Mr. James Ranson, at Stoney Creek, on the 12th inst (writes our Woodford correspondent). The deceased lady, who was 93 years of age, was born in Huntingdonshire, but on her marriage to Mr. John Joyce settled in the farming district of Conington. On the death of her husband in 1885 she, with one of her daughters, decided to come to Queensland, where other members of her family had been settled for several years. The deceased lady had a family of 12 children, seven of whom survive her. She had descendants to the number of 122, over 50 of whom are settled in Queensland.

Brisbane Courier, Tues 24 June 1913

I have been unable to verify all 12 children, although some family trees have listed up to 16. Below is a summary of the nine children I have confirmed.

- **Frederick Joyce** (1843-1877): Frederick came to Australia on the *Lobelia* in 1865, and later married Alice White – see below.

- **Thomas Joyce** (1848-1927): He is shown on the 1901 census as aged 53, an agricultural labourer, along with his wife Athalia and three children. He died in Conington in 1927.

- **Emma Joyce** (1850-?): Emma married Thomas Braybrook (a railway platelayer) in Conington in 1868. By the 1891 census they had seven children: Herbert (21), Frederick (19) Albert (15), Alice (12), John W (8), Arthur (7) and Lizzie (4m) and were living at Tempsford Bedfordshire. They were still there in 1901.

- **Alice Joyce** (1851-1923): Alice emigrated to Australia, arriving in Moreton Bay on the *Indus* in 1871, married John Benjamin Fletcher in 1874 and appears to have had twelve children. She died at Caloundra, Qld in 1923. John died in 1912.

- **Alfred Joyce** (1854-1895): Alfred was living at home in Conington and an agricultural labourer in 1871. He is listed as a deserter from the 30th Foot Corps at Fort Southwick, Hampshire in 1875. He married Sarah Payne Manning from Halifax in Yorkshire in 1883 and they left almost immediately to travel to Brisbane on the *Nairnshire* which arrived in Brisbane in July 1883. In 1889 he is listed in the *Brisbane City Directory* as being a labourer, and living at Byron Street, New Farm, and in 1891 as being a gas maker living in Villiers Street. He was still in Villiers Street in 1895. He died in Brisbane in 1895.

- **Elizabeth Ann Joyce** (1855-1936): She married a blacksmith, Randolph Mitchell, in Northowram in Halifax in 1881. She arrived in Brisbane in September 1885, on the *Merkara*, with her husband, mother, and two children. Randolph died in Woodford in 1888, and Elizabeth was married again, 6 months later, to James Ranson. She died in Gympie in 1913.

- **John William Joyce** (1857-1930): John married Hannah Briggs in 1876 in Bradford, and they seem to have lived in Yorkshire, first in Clayton, then Horton, and from 1901 onwards, Bradford. He had at least 3 children and died in Bradford in 1930. His occupation was general carter/drayman. His children all worked in the factories.

- **Susan Joyce** (1860-?): I don't think Susan ever married because she is shown as 'Joyce' and 'single' on each census I accessed. As mentioned above she had two children and moved to Bradford as a weaver.

- **Joseph Joyce** (1861-?): Joseph married Martha Moon on 24 November 1906 at St Luke's Church, Manningham – by this time he was already a widower. Judging from various family trees, it seems that his first marriage may have been to Hannah Lloyd in 1894 – she died four years later in 1898. In 1911 he was a plumber's labourer at a silk factory in Bradford, and had four children living at home, all employed in the silk factory. In total it seems he had ten children and died sometime after 1911.

Joseph White (1832-1907)

Joseph was listed as aged 20 in the 1851 census and an agricultural labourer, lodging with the Joyce family, his sister Elizabeth's family. On this census document his birthplace is listed as Conington.

Joseph White[xxviii]

At some stage between 1851 and 1859, Joseph migrated to Australia, and at this stage I have several possibilities. I surmised that the most likely port of entry was Adelaide, since he was married at Mt Gambier in 1859, but could not find any suitable matches for Adelaide.

Possible ships:

- alone; farmer at Port Phillip on *Albermarle* 7 Jul 1853
- alone; agricultural labourer from [Derby?] aged 22; to go to Francis Balfour South Geelong; arrived 2 July 1852 on the *London*
- as a convict to WA on the *Adelaide* in 1855 (doubtful, as most periods of transportation were for five years or more, and he was in Mt Gambier by 1859).

Joseph married spinster Mary Ann McMahon 13 November 1859 at Mt Gambier. This is where name confusion begins, because Mary Ann seems to have used both 'Egan' and 'McMahon' as her maiden name. She was evidently born in Clare, Ireland, and it is entirely possible that she came to Australia as a single Irish female emigrant, as with thousands of other young Irish women. Her origins are discussed in the McMahon/Egan chapter.

Several trees suggest she was born Egan and had married 'McMahon' before marrying Joseph White – but if this was the case she should not have been recorded as a 'spinster' on the marriage certificate. In addition, I can find no evidence of another marriage. Mary Ann signed her marriage certificate and Joseph made a mark, indicating he was illiterate.

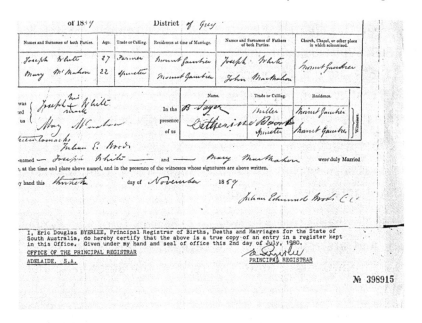

Mary Ann McMahon and Joseph White marriage certificate

At the time of their marriage, Mt Gambier was no more than a few scattered buildings surrounded by pastoral stations. The first hotel, the Mt Gambier Hotel, had been constructed in 1847, and a general store in 1850. These, along with the blacksmith's shop were all near the Cave, where fresh water was available. When they married in 1859, the population had been growing rapidly. B. Sayer, 'miller', who was a witness to Joseph and Mary Ann's marriage most likely worked at the small stone mill set up by Dr Edward Wehl in 1849.

Over the next eight years, Mary Ann and Joseph spent time in Victoria before their eventual move to Queensland, and two of their children were born during this time. Many of the family trees I reviewed seem to have guessed the birthplaces of their children and place them all in Queensland, but this is incorrect. It seems more likely that they chased work in Victoria and may also have been attracted to the gold rush at Ballarat.

Jenny Kroonstuiver

My great Grandmother Alice was born at Warenheip, near Ballarat in 1861. While Ballarat district gold prospectors were present in the 1860s and a primary school was opened, it was not until the 1870s that Warrenheip was established as a separate agricultural community, so it is quite possible that Joseph and Mary Ann were mining at this stage.

Lilley was born in 1864 at Warracknabeal, a wheatbelt town about 330 kms north-west of Melbourne.

Mercifully, thanks to the later fame of his son, George, Joseph and Mary Ann are much easier to trace after this. Following is an extract from George White's story from the Stockman's Hall of Fame:

> "In 1867 Joseph White, his wife Mary Ann and two daughters left Ballarat with the Buss family who were destined for the canefields of Bundaberg. The Whites settled on Doboy[19] Creek near Hemmant; they were very poor and several daughters married as young as sixteen. Among the children born at Hemmant was George Alfred Joseph. The family were later at Bunya Farm, upper Southpine [Strathpine] which was flooded when the river was dammed to form Lake Kurwongbah. First child born at Hemmant was George Alfred Joseph White, followed by a sister."

Joseph died on 24 January 1907 and is buried at Lutwyche Cemetery, Brisbane. Mary Ann died in January 1916 and is also buried at Lutwyche Cemetery, Brisbane.

Their children:

---

[19] 'Doboy' is also frequently referred to as 'Doughboy'.

- **Alice Pointon (born White)** (1861-1933): (our ancestor – see below) born Warrenheip, Ballarat.
- **Elizabeth Ann 'Lilley' Pointon (born White)** (1864-1927) at Warracknabeal, a wheatbelt town about 330 kms north-west of Melbourne. Elizabeth married Charles Pointon in Queensland in 1879.
- **Emma Day (born White)** (1868-1949): may have been a baby when they left Ballarat, possibly born at Ballarat but more likely Hemmant. She married William Day in Brisbane in 1885 and had eleven children.
- **Frederick John White** (1870-1945): probably born at Hemmant. Our family tree says he was 'brilliant with figures'. Frederick married Clare Ruthenberg in 1899. Son Joseph was part of the Criminal Prosecution Service at Winton by age 21 and died of meningitis at Winton without marrying. Daughter Mavis married into the Pointon family. Daughter Sue married Neil Hasemer at Mareeba and died in 1987.
- **George Alfred Joseph** (1871-1941):

Extract from the story listed in the Stockman's Hall of Fame

While still a lad, George White joined a droving plant to work in the Gulf country. It was a hard life where drinkers in the shanty pubs made sport of the boy, holding him down to pour liquor down his throat. George never drank nor smoked for the rest of his life. He spent many years in this rough country working with cattle and horses and became an expert with both.

In about 1895, he returned to south Queensland to stay with his sister, Alice Pointon, at 'Gordon Brook' while her husband, Abel, and sons, Bert and Herb, went to work on the newly-acquired 'Lilyvale' station on the Dawson River. During this time George met Emilie Constance Smith (nee Birdie). In later years he enjoyed recalling how he rode 30 miles to meet Emilie at dances in Nanango, danced the night away, and rode home to reach 'Gordon Brook' just in time to run in the horses for the day's work.

After their marriage on 28th July 1896 at Dalby, George and Emilie lived for some time at Lilyvale. A daughter Enid was born on 15th June 1897 and a son Waverley on 27th August 1905. In 1907 George was engaged by politician and big-game hunter, Arnold Weinholt, to manage Grassmere station, 100 miles south of Mitchell. Their third child, Dorothy Audrey was born there on 27 June, 1908.

A strong bond had existed between the White and Pointon families since 1879 when George's two eldest sisters, Alice and Elizabeth Ann married Pointon brothers, Abel and Charles. Now whenever they visited Brisbane the Whites stayed with Alice and Abel who had retired in 1907 to Dangore, Hamilton. Enid and her cousin Gladys Pointon attended Duporth a private school at Oxley, and occasionally Enid would bring Gladys home to 'Grassmere' for holidays. The two younger Pointon boys, Percy and Sydney worked as jackeroos on Grassmere. During almost 12 years of management, George built up the property from its unimproved state, putting in bores, fencing, and stocking the run. In 1919, after the marriage of Enid, he left Grassmere seeking a better position.

George White at Grassmere

He was offered the management of `Lake Nash' and `Carpentaria Downs', but settled for `Woomblebank' and later `Forest Vale' as they were less isolated.

Of their children, Enid married the Rev J. Cyril Flood; George married Helena Lyne and was manager of numerous stations; and Dorothy married Daniel Day, a grazier from Longreach.

- **Florence Morrow (born White)** (1875-1941): Florence married Robert James Morrow (1869-1939), from Ipswich, Qld, in 1892. They lived at Kilcoy and had six daughters and two sons. Robert was the youngest son of Irishman Robert Morrow and Lucinda Maginness who had migrated from County Donegal, Ireland with two children in 1855.

Alice Pointon (born White) (1861-1933)

My Great Grandmother Alice was born near Ballarat in 1861, and her parents are listed as Joseph White and Mary Egan in her birth records.

Alice White

At the age of sixteen, she married Frederick Joyce (who would have been about 34) in Queensland. It is possible that Frederick was a first cousin of Alice, as I believe her father Joseph and Frederick's mother Elizabeth were brother and sister. Frederick had arrived in Brisbane on the *Lobelia* in 1865, and he was a labourer living at Lytton, now a coastal suburb of Brisbane.

Sadly, less than three weeks after their marriage, Frederick was killed in an accident which also involved Joseph Kendrick, licensee for the Royal Mail Hotel, now known as the Tingalpa Hotel.

The *Queenslander* reported:

> "An accident with fatal consequences occurred at the
> Norman Creek Bridge, between eight and nine o'clock

on Wednesday evening last. It appears that Mrs. Pointon, who lives on the further side of the bridge above mentioned, had her attention attracted by hearing a sound as of some person in distress, and on looking about for the cause found a man named Joseph Kendrick in the road, suffering from an accident that had just taken place on the other side of the creek. Kendrick told her that himself and a neighbor named Frederick Joyce were returning to their homes at Tingalpa from Brisbane in a spring cart, and on approaching the bridge at Norman's Creek, they were both thrown violently out of the cart into the road. He must himself have lain some time senseless, but on recovering consciousness he called for Joyce, and received no answer. He then did his best to procure assistance, and succeeded in the manner described."

"Mr. Pointon shortly afterwards came home, and said that he had met a horse with spring-cart walking leisurely along the road, but having no one in charge. He then, as soon as possible, took up the injured men and brought them to the Brisbane Hospital; Joyce was breathing heavily, and evidently in a dying state; he lingered, however, through the night, and died about nine on Thursday morning. Kendrick bore marks of having had a good shaking, but has not been very seriously hurt, and is recovering from the effects of the spill. It is not known precisely how the accident occurred, but it is believed that the horse going down the hill at a fast pace struck violently against the post of the bridge, thus jerking the two men out on the road, without quite upsetting the cart. Deceased was

perfectly sober at the time of the accident, and was a strong, healthy young man, thirty years of age, and only married three weeks."

Observations. (1877, June 16). The Queenslander (Brisbane, Qld. 1866-1939), p. 5.

There followed a magisterial inquiry, which was also reported:

"The magisterial enquiry into the circumstances surrounding the accidental death of Frederick Joyce, who was thrown out of a cart at Norman Creek Bridge, on June 13, was held before Mr. W. H. Day, on Monday. The evidence of Dr. Thompson showed that death probably resulted from compression of the brain caused by the back of deceased's head coming in violent contact with some hard substance. The medical evidence also showed that deceased had been drinking, his breath at the time of reception at the hospital indicating this. The evidence of Joseph Kendrick who was with deceased at the time of the accident, did not directly point to the cause of the mishap, but the witness stated that the breeching broke as they were descending the decline leading to Norman Creek Bridge, which caused the spring-cart in which they were riding to swerve against the kerbing and overturn."

Alice White and Frederick Joyce[xxix]

So, Alice found herself as a widow at the age of sixteen. Her widowhood lasted for just on two years, as she married Abel Pointon (relative to the Pointons who found Frederick at the time of the accident) in July 1879 and went on to have eight children. Her story continues in the Pointon chapter.

She died aged 72, of gallstone, colic, myocarditis and heart failure, in Brisbane in 1833, and is interred in the same grave as her second daughter, Amy Pointon, her fourth son, Abel Pointon and her husband, Abel Pointon.

The McMahon/Egan Family

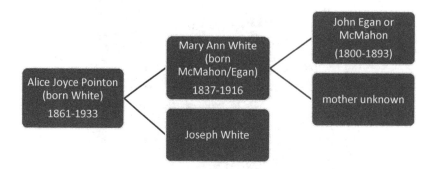

When I found family trees that had attached to John Egan three different wives, across three different continents, I knew that researching this family was going to be challenging. Add to this the fact that this family was apparently in Ireland in the mid-19th century when there was mass poverty and death, and there are thousands of 'Egans', and the job of narrowing down our ancestors became even more difficult. To further add to the complexity, our ancestor Mary Ann White appears to have used the surname 'Egan' and 'McMahon' interchangeably as birth names.

This chapter has been rewritten several times as I found new leads which sent me off in different directions.

We know that Ivy Lee's Grandmother was Mary Ann White. On her Mt Gambier marriage certificate to Joseph White, she stated her surname was 'McMahon', and that her father's name was John McMahon. However, on her daughter Alice's death certificate her maiden name is given as 'Egan'. We also know from Alice's birth certificate that Mary Ann was born in County Clare in 1838.

Various family trees seem to fall into two camps. Firstly, there are those who give her birth name as Egan and list her parents as John Egan and Elizabeth Grey. These trees list Mary Anne's birthplace as 'Creeshum', County Clare, and the birth date as 1840. However, there are no Irish birth records which are even remotely close to these details – in fact I can't even find a town called 'Creeshum' and think perhaps they meant 'Crusheen'. The main problem I have with these versions, however, is that her mother Elizabeth's birthplace is listed as Surrey, England, and I cannot imagine why she would have been in Ireland in 1838.

These trees also offer no explanation for the adoption of the surname 'McMahon'. None of them have documentary evidence of Mary Ann's birth date or place, or of the parents. However, they do have full details of Mary Ann and Joseph White's children and their death places, even though it is evident that they copied each other. This does suggest that they had some knowledge of the descendant family.

Most of the trees which use the birth name of McMahon, also give Mary Anne's birthplace as Creeshum (Crusheen?) in 1834, parents as John McMahon and Bridget Walsh, her spouse as Joseph White, but her death place as Woodford Victoria. There is a parish baptism record from Kildysart for 31 October 1834. They also list a brother, James McMahon (1833-1909) who died in Mosquito Creek, Victoria. The biggest problem I have with these trees is not just the documented death place of Victoria (when we know our Mary Ann died in Brisbane), but also the lack of information about her spouse and children, who are actually quite well publicly documented in Australia. As a result, I really do not think this is the correct Mary Ann, as anyone researching our Mary Ann would quickly have been able to identify children and movements across Australia.

After discussion with Sally Chapman and further investigating the many discrepancies among recordings of Mary Ann's name and age, I now suspect that Mary Ann may have lied about both her name and age when she married because she was underage, and then later in life felt comfortable enough to revert to her real name. If her headstone is correct, it is entirely possible that she was born closer to 1840 than 1838, which would have made her about 19 at the time of her marriage, and requiring parental permission. It would have been so much easier to simply change her date of birth and alter her father's name.

On balance, then, the birthname of 'Egan' seems to be more likely, even if some of the details in other trees are a bit questionable. However, I continued my searching using both names.

The Glencoe Massacre

To add to the confusion, my mother had notes in several places saying that the Egans were descended from the MacDonalds of the Glencoe massacre. I have no idea how she came across this information. The Glencoe massacre occurred in Scotland as part of the Jacobite uprising which began in 1689. The Massacre of Glencoe took place in Glencoe in the Highlands of Scotland on 13 February 1692. An estimated 30 members and associates of Clan MacDonald of Glencoe were killed by government forces, allegedly for failing to pledge allegiance to the new monarchs, William III of Scotland and Mary II. Why the Glencoe MacDonalds were selected is still debated; it appears to have been a combination of internal clan politics, and a reputation for lawlessness that made them an easy target.

John Egan or McMahon (c.1808-c.1893)

So, next I tried to pin down the details of the father of Mary Ann, John Egan or McMahon, and here other sources are even more confused. Other family trees had him variously married to three different women, having fathered upwards of sixteen children, having been a convict transported to Australia, and concurrently living in England and America.

Again, I began the process of elimination, and the first to go was the marriage to Mary McCarthy in Iowa in 1844. This also eliminated eight children. The reason for this was that he seemed to be concurrently having children on two different continents, and there is no suggestion anywhere else of an American connection. This was the John Egan who was supposedly the son of Patrick Egan and Mary Hickey, so I have eliminated them as possible parents as well.

Another John Egan who migrated to Iowa, was born in 1814 to Michael Egan and Bridget Egan (born McMahon). However, he seems equally unlikely to have been our ancestor.

Next to go was the John Egan, convict, transported to Australia in 1849 – a shame, because this was an interesting story. While there was certainly a convict John Egan transported to Australia from Tipperary on the *Neptune*, there is nothing to link him to our Mary Ann, and if Elizabeth Grey was his wife, then he was more likely in England at the time. In fact, I doubt Mary Anne's father ever came to Australia at all.

More difficult to eliminate was the purported marriage to Bridget Ryan in about 1830. It is possible that John Egan did marry a Bridget Ryan, and they had a son Timothy ('Thady'), and that Bridget died at Killaloe soon afterwards. But it is equally likely that this was a completely different John Egan and no relation of Mary Ann's.

So, we are left with a John Egan who was born in Ballyvannon in 1808, and at some time around 1838 married to Elizabeth Grey. However, I still have a problem reconciling an English Elizabeth Grey with a daughter's Irish birth. Some trees had an earlier daughter, Elizabeth, born in Warwickshire in 1824, but as John would have been about 16 at this time, I have discounted her. None of the trees I accessed had proof of a marriage between John and Elizabeth Grey, and the only documentary evidence was rather tenuous – some census records for 1851 and 1861, as described below. These list another daughter Margaret, born in 1847, which is a seven-year gap from Mary Ann, which is also unusual.

I found one family tree which tried to explain the name confusion. John McMahon used an alias, 'John Egan', and he married Elizabeth Grey – but no evidence! Some family trees even had Elizabeth dying in Australia but, again, with no evidence. I then searched for census records for this family.

In 1841 there were no English or Irish census records which resembled our family of John, Elizabeth and baby Mary Ann, for either name of Egan or McMahon.

However, there was an 1851 Irish census *search* record for John and Margaret McMahon, with daughter Mary Ann. Mary Ann is recorded as 'Applicant', and the family of three were living with Mr Andrew McCormack, 'borladergar', in County Tyrone.

There is a second 1851 census *search* record which may be more likely – it is for John McMahon and Maria Dooley, with daughter Mary (Applicant), living in Clare, Ireland. However, this one is marked 'not found'.

In 1851 there was an English record for John McMahon aged 30, born in Ireland, Eliza (27), Mary Ann (7), James (3) and John (1). The ages are all too young for our family, and Mary Anne's birthplace is given as Lancashire, England.

1851 census record

There is another English entry for 1851: John Egan (42), Eliza (40) — the birthplaces and ages fit with other trees, but the Mary listed is a widow of 82 and there is no Mary Ann, who would have only been 13 at the time so unlikely to already be in Australia, although she could have been in service. There is also no Margaret, the other daughter, supposedly born in 1847.

1851 census record

In the 1861 census there is an entry for John Egan (61), labourer; Elizabeth 54; and Margaret 14 living Eaton Street, Surrey. John and Elizabeth are a bit old to be our family. There is no Mary Ann, but our Mary Ann was married in Australia by this time.

1861 census record

Elizabeth Grey

But references to Elizabeth Grey are persistent, and not as easily dismissed as I first thought. Shirley Webster, who shared so much research with my mother, seemed quite sure that Mary Ann's mother was Elizabeth (Lizzie) Grey, and that she possibly had a daughter Mary in addition to Elizabeth.

The Grey name is very English and for this reason I have assumed that Elizabeth was not Irish. There certainly do not seem to be any records of Greys in and around Crusheen.

Possible birth dates for Elizabeth:

- Baptism 22 April 1821 in Dublin to William and Francis Grey
- 26 September 1803, Gloucestershire to parents William and Elizabeth Grey – this was in over 50 trees (which may simply have copied each other), but is a possibility given the proximity of Gloucestershire to Ireland. However, I can find no birth records to verify this. These trees list in some detail three children:

  o Elizabeth Egan 1824-1879, born Birmingham, Warwickshire. There is an 1841 census record for Elizabeth Egan, aged 15 living in the house of Joseph Hunt, a steel broker, but no way of verifying this is the correct person
  o Mary Ann McMahon 1840-1918 born 'Creesham'
  o Margaret Egan (1847-?), born Southwark, Surrey

- Born 26 September 1803 in Templetoughy, Tipperary, Ireland to parents William and Pheobe Grey; however generally spouse is marked as 'unknown', and there is no evident link to Mary Ann.

These record links are tenuous at best. Most have Elizabeth marrying Michael Proud, but their wedding record lists her father as Thomas Egan. There are no records which show the group as a family, nor are there any individual records.

Mary Ann White (born Egan or McMahon) (1837-1916)

At this point, I am now more inclined to accept that Mary Ann was born in Clare, Ireland, than I am to accept that her mother's name was Elizabeth Grey. This is because Ireland was specified on her daughter Alice's birth certificate, and that information would have been provided by Mary Ann herself, with no apparent reason to falsify the information.

Lots of trees had her birthplace as 'Creeshum', Clare, but there is no such place in Ireland and it is apparent that they just copied each other, so even though I suspect that they probably meant 'Crusheen', I discounted that as well.

Searching for Mary Ann's birth records from 1837 to 1845 from County Clare produced:

- Baptism 24 March 1837, to parents John McMahon and Bridget Bearse, Miltown Malbay, Clare
- Baptism 21 Feb 1837, to parents John Egan and Biddy Kenella, St Senan's. Clare
- Baptism 9 June 1838, to parents John McMahon and Margaret Marinan at Milltown Malbay
- Baptism 13 July 1843, Offaly to parents John Egan and Elizabeth Keogh, witnesses Roberth Mooney and Anne Keogh
- Baptism Feb 1838, to John McMahon and Winifred Finncane at Kildysart
- Birth May 1838, to John McMahon and Catherine McMahon at Clarecastle
- Baptism, 21 May 1838, to John McMahon and Ann Sexton, Kildysart
- Baptism 4 Oct 1838, to John McMahon and Mary O'Neill, St Senan's, Clare.

However, notes on the Crusheen websites have indicated that all birth records before 1862 have been lost, so Crusheen may still be a possibility.

Any of the above is a possibility, but without additional information we cannot narrow them down any further.

The next step was to try and work out when and how Mary Ann travelled to Australia. My suspicion is that she came out as one of the thousands of Irish orphans/single girls who came to Australia during the potato famine and into the 1850s. As she was married in 1859 in Mt Gambier, I assumed she probably arrived in Adelaide, although I searched more broadly.

Over five thousand Irish peasant girls migrated to South Australia between 1848 and 1855, many of them having spent time in Irish workhouses prior to emigrating. There were recurrent complaints about the quality of the immigrants and the increasing recruitment of Irish migrants. In particular, special selections of many young Irish women in the mid-1850s caused an adverse public reaction, though most fared well in the long run. The main sources of Irish immigrants were Clare and Tipperary, and our Mary Ann most likely came out sometime between 1855 and 1858.

There were several possible ships to Adelaide carrying a Mary Ann McMahon of the approximate correct age in the 1850s:

- 1851 – the *Osceola* – a McMahon family, so unlikely
- 1953 – the *Standard* – a McMahon family, so unlikely
- 1854 – the *Dirigo* – a Mary Ann and a James, both single – these might be the ones who ended up in Victoria

Record from the Dirigo

- 1854 – the *Sir Edward Parry* – lots of McMahons but mostly families; Mary a little too young to be ours
- 1855 – the *David Malcolm* – a possibility – Mary 18 and travelling alone

Record from the David Malcolm

- 1857 – the *Lady Ann* – a possibility, 3 McMahon women travelled from Clare. The age spread suggests they were sisters, although the age for Mary is correct.

Record from the Lady Ann

- 1858 – the *Stamboul* – a family, so unlikely.

There are also some possible matches for an arrival in NSW:

- Mary Ann McMahon arrived in 1853 as a single female aged 18 on the *America* as a domestic servant from Armagh
- Mary Egan arrived 1855 on the *Golden Era;* travelling with 'Margaret'; from Clare
- Mary McMahon arrived in 1855 on the *Gloriana;* listed as an illiterate farm servant aged 18 from Dysert, Clare; parents James and Mary both dead and seemed to be going to Biddy McMahon in Sydney, so unlikely.
- Mary McMahon arrived 1855 on the *Matoaka,* from Quin, Clare, travelling with 'Catherine' – unlikely as parents Thomas and Ann listed as living in Ireland.

Some family notes suggest the possibility of an arrival of Mary Egan (aged 14) and her sister Alice (17) in Port Phillip on the *Joshua* in February 1852. These two Irish girls do appear on the passenger list for the *Joshua*, having embarked from Plymouth. However, I have not found any further documents which link either of these two women to our families.

Mary Ann met and married Joseph White in Mt Gambier in 1859, and her story continues in the White family chapter, which is, thankfully, a little better documented.

Children of Fred and Ivy Lee

The Lee family, Christmas 1934
From left, Nancy, Ruth, Fred and Ivy nursing baby Fred

Ruth Alice Swann (born Lee)

This section was written by Ruth Swann

Ruth

My father, Fred Lee, was born on 16 February 1881 at Nanango Queensland. He was the youngest of seven sons. There was also one daughter, but she died aged four in 1870.

My mother, Ivy Lee (nee Pointon), was born on 26 April 1892 at Burlington St, East Brisbane. She was the sixth child and third daughter of Abel and Alice Pointon.

Jenny Kroonstuiver

As a young man Dad married Annie Grieve, who, sadly died about 1922. At the time she and Dad lived in 28 Sefton Avenue in Clayfield, Brisbane. Next door at Number 26 was the old family home of the Pointon family. I am not sure how many of the Pointon family were living there in 1922 but Mum was, and eight years later she, as she often told us, "hopped over the fence" to marry my father. In later years, her sister Maude, who never married, lived in the family home with a succession of nephews and nieces who stayed with her for education and work commitments.

Dad and Mum were married at Augustine's Church, Hamilton, Brisbane on 10 February 1930. Dad was almost 49 and Mum was 38 when they married. They had three children: Nancy Margaret (later Carlyon) was born on 21 January 1931; Ruth Alice (later Swann) on 17 December 1932 and Frederick Donald was born on 20 August 1934.

We lived at number 28 for five years after I was born and then Dad retired from New Zealand Loan where he was Mercantile Manager. They sold the house (it was during the depression and I believe they just about gave it away) and moved to a farm near Nanango. Dad owned three farms: two adjoining which were run by two of his brothers[20] and another some distance away run by a share farmer. A lot of members of the Lee family lived in that area – at one stage there were ten Mrs Lees in something like ten miles. As Dad and Mum were so much older when they had their family, we grew up calling all our first cousins 'Aunt' and 'Uncle' and our second cousins were more our age and more like cousins. We built a new house on one of the adjoining farms, Acacia Ridge, and my brother Fred inherited it – it now belongs to Fred's son

---

[20] In fact, the farms were run by a brother and a cousin.

Greg. Uncle Stan and Auntie Trixie had a two-storey house and I remember thinking that was the height of luxury, Uncle George and Aunty Mabel had a typical old farmhouse, it seemed old as long as I can remember it. But I digress and must go back to the first five years.

Nancy and Ruth at Sefton Avenue, 1933

My memories of those early days at Sefton Avenue are pretty sparse. I can remember there was a sleepout or sunroom at the back of the house and it had a double bed with an eiderdown. Just before one Christmas, I guess I was four or five, fascinating bumps became visible under the eiderdown and the glass door was locked. That's where Mum stored the Christmas parcels.

I can recall one time when it was Nancy's birthday and we were having a rare children's party. I can still see this little redhead (me) standing halfway down the back steps crying my heart out. Nancy and all her friends were having a game with apples tied onto the clothesline with string, and someone said I was too little to be in on it. How that hurt!

The house had a maid's room at the back. It was only used as such once as far as I can recall. That was when we three kids had mumps, measles and chickenpox one after the other when Nancy started school, and Mum was on crutches following a knee operation.

Many years later when I qualified as a Mothercraft nurse, I returned to No 28 Sefton Avenue to care for a baby girl and her three older brothers – the family name was Gole. She was the first baby girl in that house since me.

When I was about five years old I started school at a little Church of England primary school just down the road from our family home at 28 Sefton Avenue. Sefton Avenue was a loop off Sefton Road and I think our little school was on one of the corners where the avenue joined the road. I have vague memories of little navy dresses with white collars. Nancy, of course, started at the same school two years ahead of me.

Ruth and Nancy in their school uniforms

Move to Nanango

I did not attend that school for long, as Dad retired from his position with New Zealand Loan. He would have been about 60. He had two farms about 12 miles out of Nanango which were run on a shared farm basis by his brother George and cousin Stan. Uncle George, Auntie Mabel and their children Clare and Bernie lived in a small two-storied house on the second farm, Acacia Ridge, and this is where we went when we left Brisbane.

The move to the farm was a major undertaking. All our goods and chattels including furniture were taken by van to the farm. There were several places where railway bridges were over the road and every chair had to be unloaded from the top of the van because the load was too high.

Also in the load was the billiard table. The house at Acacia Ridge had been built with one room large enough for the billiard table. Later we played table tennis on the table with its six-piece cover in place. I can still see Dad's desk in one corner, Mum's desk against the wall the old time wireless with the big battery, the huge open fireplace, and the gramophone where we played the old 78 records (we had to wind it up). A school friend Ann Campbell and I gave Fred and Ronnie Yeates dancing lessons to those old records.

Fred at Nanango

The first thing we had to do when we moved to the farm was to learn to ride horses so that we could go to school. There were three little bush schools (one-teacher schools with about 10-15 pupils) each four miles from our new home, and Sandy Ridge on Barambah Road was selected for us. I think there were about ten children.

Fred, Nancy and Ruth at Acacia Ridge

Until we learnt to ride Dad would take us to school in a sulky. He was quite the 'gentleman farmer' with his little felt hat and his pipe. Many times, we would pick up the teacher who boarded with a family about a mile from the school. I remember the turn-off well, as it was right on the 'bad bend'. The teacher's name was Mary Winterburn and Dad used to say he got mixed up but more often than not he called her 'Mrs Winterbottom'.

Once we started riding, we would link up with other children after we crossed the creek and the 'first' was Ronnie Yeates. One of his brothers married Mary Winterburn and a sister married our cousin Bernie Lee. I kept in touch with Mary Yeates every Christmas until she died aged over 90.

The school had only one teacher, so they had classes for grades 1,3 5 and 7 one year and the 'preps' and 2,4,6 the next year. Nancy and I had to be put up a year to fit in which is why we finished primary school at a comparatively early age.

Sandy Ridges pupils in 1939 (back row, from left) Neville Love, Ron Yeates, — Pomerenke, Miss Gertrude Moloney (teacher), John Lee, Richard Farr, Ronald Wesener; front row, Joyce Wesener, Noela Groves, Ruth Lee, Ngari Stitchburg, Shirley Love, Marie Ewart, Nancy Lee and Elma Wesener.

Photo published in the local paper for the school reunion

We three children loved writing and interacting with the Queensland Country Life Children's page, 'the Cubby Hole', and over the years, much to our excitement, several of our letters were published. Below is my first letter, published in May 1940.

> •
>
> Acacia Ridge,
>   Nanango.
>   Dear Cousin Rob: I would like to join the Cubby Hole, if you have room in your large family for one more cousin.
>   My sister, Nancy, has joined, and I suppose Fred will want to as soon as he can write well enough. He is only five, and I am seven. I go to Sandy Ridges school, and am in third grade, with five boys. May I have "Tulip" or "Cassia" for a pen-name?— RUTH LEE.
>   There's always room for one more, Ruth—and tell Fred he'd be welcome any time. Write well enough? Pish —come up and see our hieroglyphics some time. "Cassia," eh?—All the best to everyone at Acacia Ridge.—

Ruth's Cubby Hole letter

The years 1939 to 1945 were, of course, the war years. There was petrol rationing and coupons for everything. We three kids had our own garden bed where we grew vegetables. Mum would buy the vegetables from us at shop prices – two thirds of the money had to be spent on War Savings Certificates and the balance was our pocket money. This was our war effort. I don't know how Mum and Dad managed financially. It must have been very difficult, but I can't remember any complaints. To think they managed boarding school as well. Family holidays were very rare, but I can remember once we were at Maroochydore with a family of cousins our age, but that didn't happen very often.

Family holidays were rare, usually spent at Maroochydore

At the end of year 7, a few of us went to Nanango State school to sit for the scholarship exam. I can remember the Christmas Eve when the results came out, and the relief that I had passed. I had just turned 12. Nancy had been going to school in Kingaroy where she boarded with an Aunt. The plan now was for both of us to attend Glennie Memorial School in Toowoomba, and so the hunt began for second-hand uniforms.

> *Glennie Memorial School was named after Benjamin Glennie (1812-1920), an Anglican clergyman who had arrived in Sydney in 1848. He was made deacon at Morpeth and appointed to Moreton Bay from where he made several extensive pastoral tours of the Darling Downs, including Glengallan, where he officiated at the marriages of several of our ancestors and relatives. In the early years he averaged 3,000 miles a year either on foot or by horseback. He was generous with money and by personal exertion raised the nucleus of the fund which made possible the foundation in 1908 of the Glennie School in Toowoomba.*

Jenny Kroonstuiver

It was 1945; the war years were not yet behind us. Clothing coupons governed everything we wore. In summer we had navy blue prints with detachable white collars, panama hats and short socks, with black lace-up shoes. I remember the locker rooms where several hundred girls polished their shoes. In winter we had navy blue box-pleated tunics over blue blouses and the school tie. For church and other special occasions, we had a dark navy suit with white blouse. I had never once owned a suit and although it was second-hand I loved it. I grew six inches in height that first year and must have needed complete re-outfitting that second year. The sports uniform was very daring – a brief tunic top over a blue blouse. To get the correct length we had to kneel in the floor and someone would measure up six inches. If you got it wrong, you had to undo it and hem it up again until it was right. Of course, with such a daring open side seam we wore blue cotton bloomers. *Très élégante!*

Ruth and Nancy at Glennie

I was desperately unhappy at school. I heard later that I was nearly sent home but I gradually settled in. I started in class 4B which was designed for girls who did not pass grade 7 scholarship and those like me who were too young to go up to 4A. It was a very small class the year I started; only 12 of us. The following year the school cut out grade 7 at Glennie prep and all those children passed into the senior school and 4B. That year was also the year of the polio outbreak, and we were all sent home early at the end of the year. The girl who sat next to me died from polio after she went home.

Nancy had two years at Glennie and then took up secretarial work in Kingaroy. I had one more year and passed the Junior public exam. I had always wanted to train as a mothercraft nurse and as a senior pass was not needed, I was allowed to leave at the end of 1947. My first year was spent at home while Fred went to school in Kingaroy, and I helped Mum out for that year. At weekends there were often dances in a little hall about two miles away and we often played tennis. My schooldays tennis was very mediocre but playing locally there were a couple of really good men players and only one other girl, so I had opportunity to make up a four and improved quite a bit. I would ride a bike to tennis and Dad many times drove me to the dances. When he put on his cap and lit his pipe, I knew we were going home.

Joining the work force

I was just 15 when I left boarding school and after a while at home I began training as a mothercraft nurse at the Lady Cilento home in Brisbane. After a year there looking after pre-school children, new babies and their mothers, we went on the 'cases'. There was an office in the city where our jobs were organised and it was from there that that I was told that my next job was at Retreat Station beyond Blackall and well beyond the railway line. I travelled by train and was to be met at Yaraka. We still had many miles to go and finally arrived at Retreat at about 2.00 am. I can still remember the district and feeling that I was 'home'.

Ruth (second from left), mothercraft nurse graduation

I had been booked for one month, but it wasn't long before Mary Button asked if I would stay for an extra month. I recall that as soon as I arrived, she decided we must have a tennis party so that I could meet everyone. It was there that I met the man who was to be the mainstay of my life for the next 50 years, Eric Swann.

I actually didn't see much of him at that time, as it was at least 70 miles between our stations. There was a governess at Oakham Station and two jackaroos at Retreat and we made up a foursome for the rare social events. Before I left Retreat, Win Paynter of Oakham asked me if I could go to them for a month, as her husband had to be away and she wanted to accompany him. My job would be to cook for the governess Margaret Taylor, her two little students (both girls), and Mr Callaghan, mostly known as 'Old Cally'. We shared the housework and had a lot of fun.

Retreat, 1952

Eventually I returned to the family home and more cases, mostly in and around Brisbane. Then I received a letter from Mrs Marjorie McKenzie whose husband managed Mt Marlow station to ask if I would like to be a governess the following year to their two boys. I accepted with pleasure. I hadn't quite forgotten the man I had met briefly at Retreat in the bough shed beside the tennis court.

I headed west by train to Yaraka in time for the start of the new school year. My pupils were to be Colin and Malcolm McKenzie, in grades 2 and 4 or thereabouts. Malcolm was the eldest.

My predecessor Rita Dillon had married the manager next door on Wandsworth Station which was where Eric worked as jackaroo-bookkeeper. The Wandsworth station ute was used to go to Mt Marlow nearly every weekend and so it continued as Eric visited me.

It was not long after I arrived that Eric's sister Jeannie died of leukaemia and he went home. I worried that he would not return, but he did, and all was well.

It was after the coronation ball in Isisford that we started to seriously plan our future together. The engagement ring came by post and there followed 50 years of shopping 'by post'. We had a wonderful year. Jock and Marjorie McKenzie treated me as a daughter, as they did Rita, married to Jack Greig next door. We managed correspondence lessons quite well – there was no school-of-the-air in those days. Both of the boys did well in their chosen fields as adults – Malcolm as a vet and Colin teaching, so we must have done something right.

Eric and Ruth with Jack Greig (left), 1953

Eric and I went everywhere together and took part in gymkhanas and camp drafts, tennis days and so on. The Wandsworth ute was kept busy. We got to know all the folk along the river, and as a result were offered the management of Trafalgar Station to commence after our January wedding. Trafalgar was being run by Archie McNally who had decided it was time to retire.

Late November or early December we left our jobs at Wandsworth and Mount Marlow and with Paul Weedman, jackeroo at Mt Marlow, we headed in his ute for Brisbane. We spent hours on the first day getting the ute to go and the same the second day getting it to stop (brake trouble). We eventually arrived at the Lee family farm at Nanango to introduce Eric to his future in-laws. Paul went on to Brisbane, entered a 'find the ball' picture quiz, won it and immediately sold his old ute with all its troubles and bought a new one.

Eric and Paul Weedman

After a few days Eric and I were entrusted with Mum and Dad's car and it was my turn to meet the in-laws. I have never seen so many tall people in one kitchen. Even the twelve-year old was extra tall. The baby was three and sitting in a high chair. I can remember her banging her spoon on the chair and yelling for beer while Mother Swann was trying to say grace.

We were married on 16 January 1954 in pouring rain. Thank goodness for ballerina dresses. Nancy was bridesmaid and had made my dress and her own. We didn't tell anyone where we were going the night after the wedding, so no-one could tell us that the flying boat the next morning had been delayed by heavy fog. So, there we were at the airport office, resplendent in our going away clothes, complete with one large paper bag dripping patches of confetti here and there as we went. Incidentally, there was a great deal of confetti in the hotel room we had just vacated so it was as well that we did depart at 5.00am. The flying boat eventually departed about 10.00am to take us to Hayman Island.

From left: Bill and Beat Swann, Eric and Ruth,
Ivy and Fred Lee

It was the off-season on the island; we could never have afforded it otherwise. There was a great deal of rain but it was warm rain and we walked miles in it.

We met up with another honeymoon couple, Don and Pam McGregor and an older couple with a ten-year-old son. Each day we would collect shells and put them by our cabin doors. In the morning we found that they had all walked back to the sea. Another pastime on the island was picking out the honeymooners when the flying boat arrived. Everyone would turn out to meet the boats.

Hayman Island honeymoon

When it came time to leave, we had to face a world that had experienced torrential rain. The flying boat could not get down in the bay, so we crossed to the mainland by launch. It was terribly rough and everyone except Eric was sick. All planes going south were cancelled. We managed to get on a fruit train – no amenities at all for an overnight run, and in the morning we were able to transfer to a passenger train. We got to Rockhampton to find that the railway line to Yaraka was washed away. We had to spend four days in Rocky before a train managed to get through. It was the only train to get through for six weeks.

We didn't know it at the time, but Paul Weedman had left Brisbane in his new ute with most of our worldly goods. He broke down coming out of a creek crossing and had to leave to vehicle and go for help. The creek flooded while he was away and a lot of things were soaked. Work clothes were able to be salvaged but all my photos were wrecked and the smell was awful.

Archie McNally met us at Yaraka and we finished the run to Trafalgar in his ute.

When we applied for and were given the job at Trafalgar it was understood that Archie was going to retire to the coast. He had for years had a succession of married couples, always one pair coming or another going. Now he was going to leave 'Young Eric' in charge.

Resident in the men's quarters and eating in the house with us was 'Territory George'. Neither Archie nor Territory George did any work. Archie would play patience most of the day. With the continuous rain, Archie had panicked and borrowed a bag of flour from his neighbour on the east side. Then he got another from the neighbour on the west and managed to get one through on the mail truck. So, we had three bags of flour, all weevilly, and it was a daily ritual to spread flour out on trays in the sun and encourage the little devils to leave.

The rain continued and the situation was not improved by the fact that the long drop toilet was quite a distance outside the back door – water all the way. After we arrived Archie and Territory George decided they'd stay on, effectively making us cook and cowboy. We had an awful bedroom, shared bathroom and a terrible bed. In the meantime, I was suffering from morning sickness so badly that I ended up in Blackall hospital, 200 miles away. It was becoming clear it was not the job for us. Eric was doing his day's work, then cooking for Archie and George. They rarely even got the fire going.

When word got around that we were job hunting, we were offered three overseer positions from which we chose Mt Marlow. I was in hospital when Eric packed up our few belongings and moved us into the homestead with the Mackenzies. I moved from the hospital into the tender loving care of my 'other mother'. The overseer's cottage was not quite ready – it was being built at the woolshed, about nine miles from the homestead.

The Mackenzies and Mt Marlow were the hub around which the district revolved. There were many tennis days which wound up in the evening with table tennis and a sing-a-long round the piano. The children bedded down happily in the car and many times Eric and I just got home in time to put the little ones to bed before daylight, otherwise they thought it was daylight and we'd get no sleep at all. We spent many Christmas days with the Mackenzies. Mrs Mackenzie who usually had a resident cook, made a point of inviting those who did not have a cook. This was typical of her kindness and generosity.

The cottage was very comfortable and quite adequate for our needs. We had two bedrooms with built-in cupboards, a large living-dining area, a huge bathroom with chip heater, bath and shower, and indoor toilet. At the other end of the living area was the kitchen with wood stove and kerosine fridge. There was verandah on three sides and that was where we did most of our 'living'. The kitchen end was where we had all our smokos and entertained guests. The front verandah had a table for table tennis and the other end was for sleeping.

Mt Marlow cottage 1954

Mt Marlow shearing shed 1954

Daughter number one was born in October and was followed fourteen months later by son number one. Mr Mackenzie jokingly said that if we had another baby, he'd add a bedroom to the house. He was a bit taken aback a few months later when we requested the extra room, but he was as good as his word and after suitable representations to Head Office a small room was added to the back of the house. It just held two stretchers, a cot and a small linen cupboard. Son number two arrived when his brother was 18 months old.

We had a laundry adjacent to the kitchen and, next to that, a 12V lighting plant that gave us lighting but no electrical equipment. Washing was done with the aid of a copper and draining rack and a hand wringer. The clothesline was the old-fashioned one with 'props' and it was still in use 40 years later.

Then followed six good years. The cottage, with eventually an extra room, was quite adequate for our needs. I knitted (occasionally, no great skill) and sewed to my heart's content. I made nearly everything the three children wore. In our final year Jenny started correspondence lessons; no school-of-the-air yet. I remember the first work she sent in – half a page of 'ones' and 'noughts' and not a straight line to be seen. Then in response to 'draw a picture for your teacher' she drew a snake. You've guessed it – the straightest snake you have ever seen.

We had a good social life and were included in everything that went on. Children sleeping in the car was the norm for big functions or small, with frequent checks. We made some very good friends in those Yaraka days, many of whom were lifelong friends.

David, Russell and Jenny at Mt Marlow, 1958

Sadly, the time came when we started thinking long term about saving for schooling and a growing family. The company who owned Mt Marlow had three properties and had promised us the next management that came up. But they also had three 50+ managers, so it looked as if it would be a long wait.

The search was on and eventually we found Tatala on the Nebine Creek owned by Oliver Bligh. Not a wonderful job and very drought-stricken, but a necessary step up the ladder to something better. We needed the 'manager' title.

The Mackenzies staged a wonderful farewell party for us and we were presented with a pair of red zippered suitcases. My Mum was at the farewell party, my Dad having passed away some time ago.

We arrived at Tatala to find that the previous manager and his wife had not left so it was all a bit hectic. Mr Bligh was also in residence. We moved in and took over part of the house. By the time we left two years later we were using the whole house, even what was designated as Mr Bligh's room. Our family had increased by one with the arrival of Susan.

I was entitled to a house girl or governess and it was in the capacity of governess that Margaret came to us. We had two for school by then and usually two workmen who ate separately but who had to be cooked for, so life was busy.

We had good neighbours and plenty of social outings. The house was of pisé construction, verandah all around. We mostly slept on the verandah. The lighting plant was almost in the house it was so close.

After about two years we advised Mr Bligh that we had to think about boarding school down the track and would have to look for a job that paid a little more. Just a raise would have kept us for a while. However, he didn't even answer the letter for about six weeks, at which time he sent us a telegram to tell us his son Bill was taking over in two weeks.

There we were with four children, no job and limited time to look for another. We answered every advertisement from cowboy to manager and received some interesting replies. One invited Eric to interview in Adelaide for a manager position on one of their properties in Western Australia, all expenses paid. He was in the last six. They decided we would do, and we decided they would do. Western Australia, here we come.

The sheep on the island

It rained in March of fifty-four
And the channels of the old Barcoo
Flooded out for miles around
And the sheep could not get through.

Seven thousand ewes, and lambs as well
In muddy waters stood
The overseer, as was his way
Just said "We'll need a hand".

Ken B. he made a floating bridge
To move them to higher ground
But it rained again ere the job was done
And a way could not be found.

The horsemen sent for boats to help
And hay to feed the sheep
When suddenly an idea came
"Hey fellows, what do you say?

We send the boat with a load of hay
And instead of returning bare
We could bring fifteen poor old sheep
Can we load them over there?"

So the table that the shearers used
Became a loading pier
With haybales going up one way
Sheep down, it did look queer

Then somebody thought of a motor
To save the men from toiling
And that was even better
Just to keep the billy boiling

Then one sad and sorry day
The motor it came off the boat
It fell to the bottom of the deepest hole
Manny said "I can dive, hold my coat."

So everyone tried hard to find it
But never so much as a sign
Till John P. volunteered, said he'd get it
The missing motor he'd find

So he dived and he found it did Johnny
It was heavy, heavy as lead
And he brought it right to the surface
They grabbed him by the hair of his head

They loaded the motor no trouble
While holding poor Johnny by his hair
And they finished the hay and the sheep work
And part of his head is still bare.

Barcoo flood 1954

Heading west

Having accepted and been accepted for the position of manager of three million acres of virgin station country on the western edge of the Nullarbor Plain, the next step was to get there.

With ourselves, four children aged one to seven and all necessities for a long trip, we loaded up the old Holden and set off. A friend transported the main load by ute and trailer through to Adelaide where the Company found storage until such a time as a residence was available on the station.

In the Holden we headed for Taree in NSW to Eric's family where we were to wait while Eric was installed at Kanandah. We had been warned to expect a gap of some six weeks at least.

Eric's family was perched on the top of a fairly steep hill which was covered with paspalum and constantly wet which made it rather slippery. How I hated driving up that hill, especially if the gate was closed halfway up.

As time went on and on, I made two decisions. Firstly, I asked for somewhere to live in Adelaide so that we could have Christmas as a family. Secondly, I sold the Holden, as we had arranged earlier, to a lad living next door. That put an end to driving up that dreadful hill.

The Company rented a home for us in Glenelg, and so the children and I set off on stage two. Rail bookings were made. These entailed sleeping overnight on the train three times and spending the whole day at the railway station or in a nearby park. We had one full day in Sydney and another in Melbourne. The day in Melbourne was a bit difficult as several schools were having Christmas parties and our kids felt a bit left out. We departed early for the station where we indulged in another session of people-watching before boarding the final train and arriving in Adelaide.

43 Waterloo Street, Glenelg

The Company's Adelaide office in those days was very close to the railway station so we were met by one of the partners on foot. Imagine, if you can, three tired children each carrying their own bag of necessities and a cushion with a handle on it, one sleepy baby in a pusher festooned with sundry bags, not forgetting three days of washing. By the time we walked up the short hill to the office our new employer was carrying three bags and three cushions. They had rented a house for us at 43 Waterloo Street in Glenelg and we were duly transported by car to that address.

It was a lovely old house, far more space than we needed but we were able to shut off some rooms. There were two bedrooms plus a small maid's room out the back, as well as an enormous lounge room over-full of beautiful furniture. I opened the door to the dining room, took one look and muttered "I could never use it without a butler" and decided that would be Eric's office when he came to visit. The kitchen was small but quite big enough and a small breakfast room opening into the maid's room became the most used room in the house. Sufficient furniture was available except for the baby. We had sold the cot in Queensland feeling that we could manage for a short time. Sue had other ideas and would not stay in bed on the ottoman which we had decided was the nearest thing to a cot. In a little shopping centre just around the corner there was a second-hand shop which had a cot. I recall beating the owner down by 10 shillings as long as we didn't want it delivered. So, Eric and I took one end each and carried it around the corner to this new home. Sue was no longer able to perform her little trick of going out the front gate wearing not a stitch of clothing.

When we moved into the Glenelg house there was no crockery or cutlery, so the McGregor wives went shopping for me. I was invited to go along but didn't fancy taking on central Adelaide with the four kids in tow. I was duly presented with Kanandah's first dinner set, plain pink china, 12 of everything. I was going to have to learn to think big. I was able to have one crate from our goods in storage delivered to our new home. It included my sewing machine, badly damaged in transit. I was able to trade it in on a new one and with the excellent Jetty Road shopping centre for material I was able to put my spare time to good use.

Eric came over for Christmas for a few days, but time went on and on. There was always another delay. The builder was desperately slow and disorganized. Goods were frequently delayed on rail. Time came for the new school year to start and we were not allowed to start WA correspondence, but had to enrol the three in the local state school. It was a strange feeling to stand at the front gate and wave off three little schoolies with their cut lunches and school bags. It was even stranger when Eric was over and he walked with them, carrying his briefcase as far as the tram which took him to the office in the city. I had to pinch myself to make sure it was really me, the suburban housewife.

Weeks passed and it was always 'another fortnight'. One day I received yet another telegram – the lighting plant had not arrived. I walked the six steps from the front door where I had been given the telegram, to the phone. I rang the office and said we had waited long enough. I had had enough of the city and Eric had had long enough by himself on the station. Was there a caravan or something? The General Manager said they had to get a caravan for a driller who was getting married and if Eric could find one in Kalgoorlie we could use that and a tent. He made enquiries about trains and told me we could go first class in two weeks, or economy in five days. We chose the latter and I started to pack.

In those days, economy berths were in fours, two up and two down. That suited us beautifully; Sue slept on the floor where she couldn't fall out. Our crate of goods was repacked, including the pink dinner set, twelve of everything, but not my brand-new sewing machine. On advice from the Singer agent, it went in its very own case with us. Goods for storage went back to store. Little did we realize that though we left Adelaide in May, we would not move into the house, even then partially finished, until Christmas Eve.

We had rain for the whole week before we left. House cleaning was going to be a problem, so I followed local custom and advertised for someone to do it after we moved out. It was the next-door neighbour who applied, and I can hear her to this day saying "It'll cost you two pound, love". It was the best two pounds I ever spent as I ended up with a heavy cold and every child in the district came to say goodbye and play in this big empty house.

It was arranged that we would be driven to Port Augusta to board the Trans Train, saving us having to change trains as would be the case if we boarded in Adelaide. It was easier this time as the children were all six months older and each carried his or her cushion and bag with a bit less complaining. We still had the pusher. The cot, being too useful to part with, went to storage with the rest of the gear.

Our kind and helpful General Manager, who was to become a lifelong friend, duly loaded us and our 21 pieces of assorted luggage onto the train on what was to be the first of a great many journeys across the Nullarbor to Naretha Siding.

Naretha railway siding in 1963

On our arrival at Naretha the next afternoon we were met by Eric in the builder's station wagon. I counted the children. OK. I counted the pieces of luggage. Only 19. The guard had another look in the van. "Nothing here lady". I counted again, Still 19. He looked again. Then I realised the boys were wearing their school bags. "That's OK. Thank you very much." Eric insisted I had undone six months of good will he had established with the railways!

So, we left Naretha for the 'homestead.' First, we had to go via the Lime Kilns to see if there were any telegrams. They were taking care of all two-way radio traffic until our own radio was set up.

Eventually we reached home. Eric had indeed bought a second-hand caravan but a wet trip from Kalgoorlie had taken three days and left it rather muddy inside and out. The rain also revealed that the caravan leaked very badly. The caravan had been towed into a position near the centre of what became known as 'The Hill'. It was not too far from the engine shed – the engine gave us 240V power when it was running. A tree beside the caravan door became my kitchen extension, and anything that would hang on a nail was conveniently hung on it. A few steps further on was the entrance to the tent. The tent was just big enough to hold four cyclone stretchers. To make the beds Jenny and I would stand one at the head, one at the foot, make a bed and move it over, make the next and move it over and so on, repeated in the other direction the next day. The open fire was nearby. It provided all our hot water and there was usually a camp oven on as the stove in the van only had two burners and a small oven. Bathing was done in a tin tub and the children and me had to be all clean by 4.45pm. This was a land with no twilight. By 5.00pm it was well and truly dark.

First camp at Kanandah

We had some rain every day but two for six weeks after our arrival. Despite the inconvenience we did have an outstanding year for wildflowers, and for grass and grass seeds, but that's another story.

The caravan which Eric brought out from Kalgoorlie had to serve as homestead from May until July in 1963. At one end was a wide bench which held the two-way radio, office equipment etc. The double bed wasn't much bigger than an average caravan bunk. A leaking window meant that many times half the bed was damp. The stove, two burners and a small oven was opposite the door. At the other end of the van was a built-in seat serving two sides of a good-sized table. This was our meal table. The most we ever fed in the van was ten, nine at the table, very jammed up, and Sue in the pusher with her plate on a powdered milk tin between her knees.

The table also served as a schoolroom for the older three. When we arrived, we had already arranged for WA correspondence lessons to be sent and this was just as well, as SA and WA school holidays did not coincide. While we left SA just as their holidays were starting, we arrived in WA ready to start the new school term, so we were into lessons on day one.

Altogether, we spent seven weeks in the caravan and tent. The building team gradually made things a little easier. First the toilet for the men's quarters was made serviceable – two toilets and a handbasin in one small room with no roof. The toilets had a partition between them but no doors. With some dozen or so men and various women and children it was interesting to say the least. Later the tin tub for bathing was replaced by the men's bathroom. Ladies had to be all finished by the time the men finished work, then it was their turn. This room had two showers, two handbasins and room for the washing machine which had moved from beside the caravan.

251

Some time later, what became known as the cook's bathroom was built and this was designated for the women. It had one shower, toilet and handbasin. All the buildings were serviced by the old-style hot water system, a 44-gallon drum with a fire underneath.

This type of hot water system was to serve us well for the nearly 30 years we were at Kanandah.

Our house was still unfinished, as was the overseer's house, the men's quarters and the shed. It was becoming increasingly obvious that the staff needed a cook. We moved into the quarters in July and had the use of the kitchen or dining room but never both. We had just a small gas stove. Eventually we set a date in October on which I would start cooking for the men and would have use of kitchen and dining room. That job snowballed with the emergency shearing and for a time I cooked for 30 people.

We moved out of the quarters on Christmas Eve into the homestead which was eventually fully finished the next May.

Kanandah homestead at the end of 1963

Shopping

When we lived on Mt Marlow, Yaraka was our nearest town. As far as shops go there was only one general store run by Mrs Price. We got our weekly order on the mail truck. Mrs Price ran the post office and telephone exchange as well. There was a Mr Price (Old Stan) who I think officially ran the store but my memories always have Mrs Price in that role.

There were shops aplenty in Blackall, 150 miles up the railway line, and we got there periodically. In those times in the pastoral industry, staff were usually paid a salary or an award wage, and were either found or unfound. 'Unfound' meant you paid for your own food but were allowed meat and sometimes milk. I did my own ordering from Mrs Price and there was also the station storeroom. The system must have worked as I don't remember any hassles. Mrs McKenzie used to send us milk, usually in rum bottles. That's how Grandma came to serve the kids' breakfast with rum instead of milk.

Morven was our next town, whilst at Tatala, with still only one store. Again, we were fully found. Perishables came from Morven via the mail truck. For basic stores I had to send the order to the owner of the property and he would get them cheaper and send them out when he could. He also took the opportunity to cut the list if he thought I didn't need it. I can recall six tins of sweet corn being altered to four. I don't think he realized that I simply added what he had cancelled to the Morven order. Also on the shopping scene was the occasional visit from a hawker with a great variety of goods in his van.

When we moved to Western Australia, we were opening up new country and much of what we did was done the Queensland way. One major difference was that all staff were on an unfound basis. It was a bit hard to get used to, but we adapted. While we had a cook in the men's quarters, they were all 'found' but quite a few of the men thought they were better off doing their own meals although a lot of them didn't eat properly. Breakfast might be a can of Coke and a cigarette.

Shopping at Kanandah had to be worked out as we went along. First there was the Tea and Sugar train which as well as carrying the bulk of our freight, had a grocery shop and a butcher's van. The Tea and Sugar came through once a week, but you could never be quite sure when. Many times the whole staff spent a whole day at the siding because they had to get food. It became imperative to start a station store and to kill our own sheep. We received great assistance from various shops in Kalgoorlie. Over the years Sheed's Store would send out our newspapers and any small parcels from other places in town (too small and easily lost by the railway staff). I kept the station store and cold room well stocked with anything anybody wanted. Initially, all ordering was done by mail or telegram. Years later we got the phone on and eventually a fax machine. That was wonderful for big orders for 10 or 20 people.

Shopping for clothes and household goods had to be done when one was in town or on holiday. We usually had a list from staff members as well. Staff never had any cash. All transactions and to go through the books which over time made a lot of extra work. We did a great deal of shopping from catalogues and advertisements. Many people were very helpful.

'The Hill' homestead complex, taken in the late 1960s

This was the last of Ruth's recorded story. Ruth and Eric spent the next 29 years on Kanandah, before finally retiring to Esperance on the south coast of WA. Mum contributed extensively to 'A Place in the West', the story of the founding of Kanandah published by my father. As her Parkinson's progressed, most of her writing was in verse. Mum had always been a talented poet, able to construct a verse about any event in minutes, and some of this poetry appears elsewhere in this book. She died at the age of 80 in 2013. Eric died three years later, in 2016.

The sausage machine

Everyone gather down at Gary's place
Going to make sausages. What a job to face.
All the mince is ready, beef and mutton mixed
Please hold the scales while we get the weighing fixed.

Twenty-five pounds it looks like to me
Add three of seasoning and what do we see?
All thick and mushy, and freezing cold too
Now add the water like Reg used to do.

Sort out the skins now, long skins are best
Hope there's no holes in 'em, mince is quite a test.
Meat on the chair there, is the mincer ready?
Your turn first Fred, turn it nice and steady.

We should have a motor. "No way" says Fred
"There'd be a few more fingers gone dead".
Eric did his little bit, turning round and round
Then we saw Bob though he hadn't made a sound

So he took his turn next in line
Someone put the mince in, snags came out fine.
"Clean it out' says Maureen. "No need" says hubby
"What we need now is another cold stubby."
Keep on turning, each has a go

"Clean it out" says Maureen. "Where did Fred go?"
Still more mince left, getting pretty slow
Hands getting tired, beer's getting low.

In walks Fred with electric drill
Fred'll fix it, he's no dill.
Away we go now, racing round and round
Going like crazy; terrible sound.

"Clean it out" says Maureen. "Yes, good thought.
Should have said so earlier; sinews get caught."
Nice clean mincer, drill going mad
Sausages came racing, that's not bad!

Ruth tied 'em all in knots, thin ones and fat
Long ones and short ones twisted like that.
Don't go too fast, they'll all fall apart
Sausage mince everywhere, back to the start.

We got it all finished and cleaned up the mess
Washed up the mincer, Gary did the rest,
Pretty good bangers, though we say it ourself
Jolly nice flavour and good for your health.

Problem Jackaroos

Peter came from England
Away across the sea
Thought he'd get himself a job
A mechanic he would be.

But mechanic's jobs were hard to find
And Peter had to wait
Until his box of tools arrived
On some dim future date.

So in meantime here at Fred's
There's plenty of work to do
And Peter found himself roped in
As a Pommy Jackaroo.

Her rode the bike for miles and miles
'Cross stones and grass and burrs
His biggest worry is the 'flats'
How often that occurs!

Now bikes can be quite moody
When you try to change their wheels
And if the nasty thing won't go
Then Pete takes to his heels.

But it isn't very easy
Chasing twenty thousand sheep
Well, maybe he exaggerates
But he counted in his sleep.

It isn't very easy,
As I know you understand
When flatties dog you every day
As you ride across the land.

So he wouldn't stay a jackaroo
If we asked on bended knee
He wants a job where he needs no wheels
And knocks off in time for tea.

Nancy Margaret Carlyon (born Lee)

With thanks to her children, Craig, Yvette and Grant, who contributed this section.

Nancy

The eldest of the three Lee children, Nancy was born on 21 January 1931 in Wooloowin, one of the northern suburbs of Brisbane, Australia. She was baptised on 7 March 1931 at St Augustine's in Hamilton in Brisbane. The family lived nearby in Sefton Avenue in Clayfield. Nancy first started school at the Church of England Primary School near the family home in Sefton Avenue. Her younger sister Ruth joined her at the school two years later.

From left: Ruth, Fred, Nancy, taken in the late 1930s

In 1937 the family sold their Sefton Avenue home and moved to a farm near Nanango.

Upon moving to Nanango, the girls changed schools to the one teacher school at Sandy Ridge on Barambah Road. Being in the country, the girls rode their horses to school as soon as they were able.

At the end of year 7, Nancy moved to Kingaroy to attend school. During the next two years she lived with an Aunt. Once Ruth graduated from Year 7, both girls attended Glennie Memorial School in Toowoomba. Nancy spent two years at Glennie before returning to Kingaroy to take up secretarial work. Nancy's grades for the Junior Public Certificate held in November 1944 were:

- English C
- English History C

- Geography C
- Arithmetic A
- Algebra A
- Geometry B
- Bookkeeping and business methods B.

Her children think that Nancy may have attended St. Margaret's in Brisbane for a short time but have no record of this.

The University of Queensland awarded her Junior Certificate on 31 January 1945. Few students went on to further study at that time. In addition to her school achievements, Nancy could touch type, take shorthand and speak pidgin English.

Nancy, taken in the late 1940s

In Kingaroy, Nancy worked for the local Mazda agency and for Radio 4SB. In 1954, she moved to Brisbane where she and her friends Dot Huff (later Wilson) and Jean Green lived in a flat in East Brisbane. The three young ladies later shared a house in the same area. In 1956, Nancy moved to Mt. Isa where she met her friend Marion Pearce. They both worked in the secretarial pool for Mt. Isa Mines.

One fateful Sunday afternoon, Nancy and Marion went to the local swimming pool for an afternoon of sun and relaxation. They were sitting peacefully when some boisterous young men diving into the pool splashed Nancy with water. The chief culprit was honourable enough to apologise. His name was William Ronald (Ron) Carlyon. Ron was working as a metallurgical engineer for Mt. Isa Mines. He was born in Ballarat in Victoria and after spending 1952 to 1954 working in Lae in New Guinea he had moved to Mt Isa to work in the mines.

Love blossomed and Nancy and Ron were married on 27 December 1958 in the Church of St. Augustine in Hamilton, Brisbane where Nancy had been baptised 27 years earlier. The witnesses at the wedding were Eugene Charles (Charlie) Gavan and Marion Innis Pearce. Ron's partner in crime on the day of the infamous dive bombing and splashing was none other than Charlie Gavan who later married Marion.

Nancy and Ron, wedding day 1958

Nancy and Ron returned to work in Mt. Isa after the wedding and a short honeymoon on the Great Barrier Reef. The couple's first child, Craig Michael, was born on 9 February 1961. They were blessed with a daughter, Yvette Leanne (now Dawson) on 12 November 1962. In late 1963, the young family packed up their possessions and left Mt. Isa for Newcastle in New South Wales. It was there that their third child, Grant Darryn, was born on 4 March 1964.

From left: Yvette, Grant, Craig

The family lived at 1 Moulden Street, Speers Point, in Newcastle. The house was located at the top of a steep hill next to Lake Macquarie and was the scene of many accidents and minor medical emergencies, primarily involving two young boys (a trait clearly inherited from their father). Craig was enrolled in Speers Point Primary School, where he attended kindergarten, Years 1 and 2. Yvette attended kindergarten at the same school.

Unfortunately, Nancy suffered from hay fever and the Newcastle spring caused major allergies. In January 1968 the family moved to Brisbane, initially renting a house in Disraeli Street, Indooroopilly. Craig was enrolled in the nearby Indooroopilly State

Jenny Kroonstuiver

School and Yvette at St. Aiden's in Chelmer. Ron commenced work at Sargent's, a steel fabrication factory in Sherwood. Grant initially attended Hillsdon kindergarten and started in Year 1 at Indooroopilly State School in 1969. Many years later Yvette would live in the house next door to Hillsdon kindergarten. Nancy managed the busy household.

After six months renting in Disraeli St, Nancy and Ron purchased 28 Musgrave St, Fig Tree Pocket. The house was on half an acre giving plenty of room for the children to run around. Nancy joined the Indooroopilly State School P&C and as was her habit, worked extremely hard to make the committee work well. Ron soon convinced her that if she was going to work so hard, she might as well get paid for it.

Carlyon family

In early 1970, Nancy started working for Magazine Art in their Queensland Office in Brunswick Street, Fortitude Valley. Magazine Art were a specialist magazine publisher headquartered in Melbourne and Nancy quickly rose to the position of Queensland

264

Manager. In December 1972, the office building where they worked, mysteriously burnt down. Fraud was suspected, however never proven. All that survived in the Magazine Art Office was the fire-proof safe, which fortunately, protected the company's most valuable records. At the time of writing (2021), the land upon which the office building once sat had not been redeveloped despite being 1 kilometre from the centre of Australia's third largest city. It is possible that this fire was linked to the 1973 Whiskey Au Go-Go fire and massacre.

Magazine Art moved to a new office nearby in Ann St, where Nancy continued to manage the state office. In 1975, she was invited to join the Board of Directors of Magazine Art.

While managing Magazine Art, Nancy had the honour of publishing one of her mother's paintings on the cover of the CWA's 1974 Annual Report. The painting used on this cover is shown in her mother Ivy's story in the Pointon chapter.

Nancy had an exciting 1970. In addition to her starting at Magazine Art, Ron bought a winning ticket in a 'Golden Casket' (the Queensland lottery), where they won a $15,000 first prize. Privacy was not as valued at that time, as on the afternoon of the win, three different banks arrived at the house to tell Nancy that they had won the lottery (and to offer their banking services). The win allowed the family to pay off their mortgage and to build a 40'x20' swimming pool. Home swimming pools were quite a luxury in the early 1970s. Also, in 1970, Ron became the Dry Mill Superintendent at Consolidated Rutile in Meeandah in Brisbane.

In 1972, Craig was enrolled at Church of England Grammar School (Churchie) in East Brisbane near where Nancy first lived with her 2 friends almost 20 years earlier. Grant joined Craig at Churchie in 1975. Yvette enrolled at Brisbane Girls Grammar in 1975.

One of the most important aspects of Nancy's life was supporting her three children. She went to every swimming carnival and gymnastic event in which the children competed, she taught Yvette to sew on her sewing machine (which Yvette still uses) and she took a keen interest in each child's academic progress. Nancy's efforts certainly paid off for all three children. Craig went on to University. He now has three University degrees, a B.A. (Psych) from Queensland University, a B. Bus (Mgmt.) from Queensland University of Technology and an MBA from Northwestern University of Chicago and Hong Kong University of Science and Technology. Yvette graduated from Queensland University with a Bachelor of Physiotherapy. Grant went on to attend the Australian Institute of Sport where he represented Australia in Gymnastics at many world events. He also has a Bachelor of Applied Science (Sports Science) from the University of Canberra.

In the early 1970's Marion and Charlie Gavan purchased a convenience store at Massey Street, Ascot, where the Gavans, Nancy, Ron and the children spent many a Sunday evening talking, laughing and solving the problems of the world. Most Christmases were spent with Dot and Bill Wilson and their three children at their home in Camp Hill.

By the early 1980's all three children had left home and in 1984, Nancy and Ron's marriage ended in divorce. Nancy was still working for Magazine Art however at the end of 1985 she closed the Brisbane office and moved to Melbourne. Nancy continued to work for Magazine Art in Melbourne until the late 1980's, and lived in an apartment on the Nepean Highway in Brighton East.

Nancy in later years

Nancy's first grandchild, Aimee Louise Dawson, was born on 5 July 1989. Nancy was overjoyed when she met Aimee during Yvette and her husband Mark's trip around Australia in 1989.

Nancy however was in failing health and she passed away on 16 February 1991 soon after her 60th birthday.

After her passing, five more grandchildren were born. Toby Lee Dawson on 24 August 1991, Clancy Robert Dawson on 24 January 1995 (Yvette's sons), identical twins Zoe Ellen Carlyon and Ilke Louise Carlyon on 24 June 1996 (Craig's daughters) and Charlie-Rose Carlyon on 4 August 2005 (Grant's daughter). At the time of writing Nancy also had three Great Grandchildren.

Frederick Donald Lee

With thanks to his children, Lyndy, Greg and Debbie, who contributed to this section

Fred

Born In 1934 at Sefton Avenue in Brisbane, Fred was the youngest son of Fred and Ivy Lee. He was still a baby when the family moved to the farm at Nanango, so most of his early memories would have been of the farm where he lived for most of his life.

Ruth and her older sister Nancy were very close as children and, not surprisingly, most of Ruth's memories relate to their friendship: Fred receives only the occasional mention. However, like his sisters, Fred was a correspondent with the 'Cubby Hole', as seen from the following letter published in 1940:

DEAR COUSINS: Four new cousins enter the family circle, and we are pleased to welcome them. Loud applause. Fred Lee, of Acacia Ridge, Nanango; Janet McCallum, of Boxthorne, Pittsworth; Glen Zeisemer, of Bongeen, Oakey; and Roy Zeisemer, Glen's brother. Lots of requests for pen-pals, cousins, so I can see you getting busy writing letters. Happy days to you all, and cheerio.—COUSIN ROB.

Acacia Ridge,
Nanango.

Dear Cousin Rob: I would like to join the Cubby Hole. I go to school. I am in prep. two. We have a tennis court. We are learning to play tennis. We live on a hill and have a lovely view.—FRED. LEE.

Fred., we are very, very happy to have you in the Cubby Hole. How is the tennis? All the best!—C.R.

Cubby Hole letter

Fred and his father, at Acacia Ridge

Acacia Ridge was a dairy farm in the early days, so Fred's life as a young teenager would have been dictated by the routine of milking, which continued well into his adult life.

At one stage he must have been admitted to either cadets or part of the land army as the photo below shows him in uniform.

Fred on the front steps of Acacia Ridge

During the 1950s he was at nearby Ridgemere, also part of the Lee family holdings, and he was still there in 1958, two years after his father's death. Ridgmere is immediately to the south of Acacia Ridge. Fred may have been managing Acacia Ridge from Ridgemere, though, because there is no-one listed at Acacia Ridge on the electoral roll for that year, or for the next few years.

At the time of his marriage to Valerie Muir at Nanango in 1954, Fred was still at Ridgemere. They had three children: Lyndy (b. 1955), Greg (b. 1956) and Debbie (b. 1958).

Marriage of Fred Lee and Valerie Muir, 1954
From left: Fred and Ivy Lee, Fred and Valerie,
Kathleen and David Muir

At the time his father moved to Acacia Ridge in 1930s, dairying was the most widely spread agricultural industry in Queensland, and there were five co-operative butter factories in the South Burnett, including at Nanango (since 1906). When Fred took over the farm in the 1950s, the decline of dairying had already begun as butter prices dropped, a decline that continued well into the 1970s. Butter production ended in Nanango in 1977 and the factory closed in 1986, and it was around this time that Fred also ceased dairy production at Acacia Ridge.

From left: Greg, Lyndy and Debbie

Although he continued some cropping, an outside income was also needed, and Fred turned his hand to stock buying and became well known as a stock buyer in the South Burnett area. Together with his son Greg, he set up a successful cattle breeding enterprise, which Greg is still running.

Valerie died of cancer, aged 52, in 1985 and is buried at Nanango. Three years later, Fred married again, although this ended in divorce. It was during this time that the house was renovated to include more modern bathroom and kitchen facilities.

Fred was the quintessential farmer, a man of few words and always quiet and reserved, but at the same time a devoted family man. In his later years, Fred had a wonderful time with his eight grandchildren and four great grandchildren. He was especially close to Becc, Greg's eldest daughter and Fred's first grandchild.

Fred died at Nanango, aged 71, in 2005.

Fred Lee, in 2004

*Acacia Ridge homestead, first built by Frederick Septimus
Lee and gradually modified over the years.*

The Descendants

In writing this book I elected to stop with the children of Ivy and Fred Lee, my parents' generation, as most of the later Lee and Pointon descendants are still living and I did not wish to impinge upon their privacy.

That said, in recent years there have been some concerted efforts to document the family descendants. Most notable has been the work of Don Morris, a descendant of Charles Pointon, who put together an extensive family tree of current Pointon descendants in about 2006. I have referred frequently to the pages and pages of research he compiled, even though he freely admitted at the time that there were many gaps. Documenting descendants is so much more challenging than writing about ancestors, because the situation changes so quickly with additional births and deaths, so I am deeply indebted to the efforts of Don Morris.

The Fred and Ivy Lee descendants were separated for many years by the tyranny of distance to the point where many of the cousins from my generation had minimal contact for over 50 years. It was not until I began researching for this book that we reconnected. Many of us are now grandparents ourselves and we have been learning as much about each other as our heritage.

Nancy and Ron Carlyon's children:

- Craig
- Yvette
- Grant

Ruth and Eric Swann's Children:

- Jeannette (Jenny)
- David (died in 1973)

- Russell
- Susan (died in 2004)

Fred and Violet Lee's children:

- Lyndy
- Gregory
- Deborah

As DNA tracing is used more and more for genealogical purposes, we frequently learn of additional possible third and fourth cousins. At the time of writing this book, very few of the Lee/Pointon descendants had shared DNA results, but this technology has the potential to resolve many of the mysteries and blockages I encountered. Perhaps in the future our own descendants will be able to fill the gaps.

My own DNA ethnicity estimate confirms the substantial Scottish and English heritage reflected in this book, as well as in my father's heritage. A little more surprising is the significant north-western Europe component which suggests a far greater Viking and Norwegian heritage than I have yet managed to establish.

About The Author

Jenny Kroonstuiver is the daughter of Ruth and Eric Swann, and a granddaughter of Fred Lee and Ivy Pointon. Born in the 1950s, she spent her childhood living on pastoral stations firstly in western Queensland and then on the Nullarbor Plain in Western Australia. Jenny trained as a teacher and spent several years teaching in country areas of the Northern Territory and Queensland, before returning to Kalgoorlie in the 1980s. After a short-lived marriage, she raised her four children alone, continuing to work in the broader education sector. From 2004, she took up a role managing the national training system for the Australian meat industry, a role she held until her retirement in 2020. Since then, she has been researching family history and this is her third book.

Image Credits

---

[i] Public domain - This image is of Australian origin and is now in the public domain because its term of copyright has expired. According to the Australian Copyright Council (ACC), ACC Information Sheet G023v17 (Duration of copyright) (August 2014).

[ii] Item is held by John Oxley Library, State Library of Queensland., Public Domain, https://commons.wikimedia.org/w/index.php?curid=12403092

[iii] With thanks to Sally Chapman

[iv] Software License. PAT is free software. Copyright © 2010, 2013 by Ian Macky.(Maps on this site, demonstrating PAT, are all public domain) https://ian.macky.net/pat/license.html

[v] Reproduced with permission from Islington Local History Centrehttps://www.localbuyersclub.com/single-post/islingtonhistory

[vi] http://spankingart.org/wiki/File:A_Peep_into_the_Blue_Coat_School.jpg This image has been released into the public domain by the copyright holder, its copyright has expired, or it is ineligible for copyright. This applies worldwide.

[vii] Reproduced with permission from Mac Gordon http://www.manar.org.uk/australiangordons.htm

[viii] © Copyright Clive Wooliscroft and licensed for reuse under this Creative Commons Licence.Content is available under Creative Commons Attribution Share Alike unless otherwise noted.

[ix] Source: https://www.rootschat.com/forum/index.php?topic=615747.9

[x] With thanks to Sally Chapman

[xi] With thanks to Sally Chapman. The reference to brothers John and Joseph was a notation by Shirley Webster, but cannot be confirmed.

[xii] With thanks to Sally Chapman

[xiii] With thanks to Sally Chapman

[xiv] With thanks to Sally Chapman

[xv] Reproduced with permission from Who's Who in Australia, published by Mediality Pty Ltd

---

[xvi] With thanks to Sally Chapman

[xvii] Photo reproduced courtesy of Brisbane City Council

[xviii] With thanks to Sally Chapman

[xix] With thanks to Sally Chapman

[xx] With thanks to Sally Chapman

[xxi] With thanks to Sally Chapman

[xxii] With thanks to Sally Chapman

[xxiii] With thanks to Sally Chapman

[xxiv] With thanks to Sally Chapman

[xxv] With thanks to Sally Chapman

[xxvi] With thanks to Yvette Dawson

[xxvii] This file is made available under the Creative Commons CC0 1.0 Universal Public Domain Dedication. https://commons.wikimedia.org/wiki/File:St._Swithun_church,_Cheswardine.jpg

[xxviii] With thanks to Sally Chapman

[xxix] With thanks to Sally Chapman

CPSIA information can be obtained
at www.ICGtesting.com
Printed in the USA
LVHW052356310521
689000LV00016B/1072

9 781922 628213